BLACKS IN

DEEP SNOW

Colin A. Thomson

BLACKS IN

DEEP SNOW

Black Pioneers in Canada

J.M. Dent & Sons (Canada) Limited

ACKNOWLEDGEMENTS

Acknowledgement is gladly made to the following for permission to reproduce copyright material: Quotations from Daniel Williams (p. 65) and "Judicial Memorandum" (p. 65) from *The Wild North Land* by William Francis Butler, published by Hurtig, Edmonton; "We Wear the Mask" (p. 93) from *The Complete Poems of Paul Laurence Dunbar* published by Dodd, Mead & Co., New York.

The following original sources are also acknowledged: A. G. Garrioch, *A Hatchet Mark in Duplicate*, Toronto, Ryerson Press, ca. 1929, pp. 115-116 for "Banjo Mike" McGinnis' defense of Daniel Williams (p. 63); Agnes C. Laut, *The Canadian Commonwealth*, New York, The Chautauqua Press, 1917, pp. 112, 120-124, 131, 137-140 for quotations from Agnes C. Laut.

Every reasonable effort has been made to ensure that acknowledgements for quoted material and photographs are complete and correct. Apology is made for any inadvertent errors or omissions.

Particular thanks are extended to my University of Lethbridge colleagues and students who encouraged me in this work, and to Miss Nettie Ware of Vulcan, Alberta, Mr. J. D. Edwards of Edmonton, Alberta, Mr. Jerrold Armstrong of Kinistino, Saskatchewan, and Dr. George H. Zieber of Lethbridge. The courtesy and co-operation of the following organizations and institutions are gratefully acknowledged: the Glenbow-Alberta Institute, the *Melfort Journal* and the Provincial Archives of Saskatchewan and Alberta.

Myrna Greene of the University of Lethbridge Educational Research Centre made many helpful suggestions and typists Edith Craig, Beth Ronaghan and Gail McGregor mysteriously deciphered my hand-written notes. For his inspiration I must thank one of Canada's gracious gentlemen, Dr. William Pearly Oliver of Halifax, Nova Scotia — black educator, clergyman, leader and friend.

TABLE OF CONTENTS

PREFACE

Columbus' crew included, among others, a Jew, an Irishman, an Englishman, a Pole, and a Black — the future New World in microcosm.

Black people have lived in the "New World" as long as most non-Whites. In Canada, the beginning of black settlement coincides with the establishment of Port Royal, the French outpost in what is now Nova Scotia.

For two hundred years black Canadians were an enslaved people — bought and sold at auctions, publicly whipped, and, in at least one instance, tortured to death. After 1833, when slavery was abolished within the British Empire, black Canadians remained a people in bondage. For the next century their story became one of sustained persecution by a country determined to "keep Canada white". Only recently have Canadian Blacks been able to throw off their chains. But the shackles' scars remain.

The emphasis in this book is on black settlement in Canada's pioneer West. However, Blacks in all parts of Canada are considered. At no time in Canadian history has the black population exceeded two percent of the total population. At the same time, that seemingly negligible fraction has been hounded by an overwhelmingly dominant white Canadian society. Apart from its intrinsic worth, then, black Canadian history is valuable for what it reveals about that dominant society.

To talk of white racism in Canada does not mean that everyone who is white believes that the white person possesses inborn superiority. It does mean that Canadian society operates as though this were the case; that the nature of our society is the same as if this belief were indeed shared by most Whites.

The term *Black* rather than *Afro-American*, *Coloured* or *Negro* is used throughout this book. Exceptions are to be found in certain quotations. The terms *Canada* and the *United States* refer to the areas presently incorporated by those nations. Exceptions are made only where necessary. *New France* refers to the French colony prior to 1763. Until 1841, today's Ontario was *Upper Canada* and present-day Quebec was *Lower Canada*. From 1841 to 1867, they were *Canada East* and *Canada West* respectively.

Colin A. Thomson,

University of Lethbridge

SLAVERY'S CHILDREN

The Ignoble Institution

Slavery, humanity's most ignoble institution, is as old as inhumanity itself. Slavery, said Plato, is a system of the most complete injustice. That "system of outrage and robbery," to use Socrates' words, has to today continued to be part of the human experience. As slave owner Thomas Jefferson later suggested, it is "the most unremitting despotism on the one part, and degrading submission on the other". Many ancient civilizations were based on slavery. In ancient Greece, for example, slavery was deeply imbedded in the social order by the time (eighth century B. C.) of Homer. The "glory that was Greece" was often "polished by slaves". The chief schools of Greek philosophical thought largely accepted slavery as a necessary part of life. Justification was based on the "natural inferiority" of most people. Aristotle in his *Economics* discussed the correct treatment of the "natural slave":

> Three things make up the life of the slave: work,
> punishment and food. To give them food but no
> punishment and no work makes them insolent; and
> that they should have work and punishment but no
> food is tyrannical and destroys their efficiency. It
> remains therefore to give them work and sufficient
> food; for it is impossible to rule over slaves without
> offering rewards, and a slave's reward is his food.

The Epicureans did not condemn slavery. Stoicism looked at
slavery as a mere accident of existence. A person could practise
Stoicism whether free or slave. No person should complain
about being a slave since he could always free himself by
suicide. Fifth century B.C. Athens, the so-called home of
democracy, was also a home for slavery.

Later in Rome slaves were considered part of the spoils of
war. Indeed, the enslavement of prisoners was thought to be a
step forward in civilization from the earlier practice of killing
them. Roman slaves provided much of the agricultural labour.
Slaves became artisans and gladiators and victims to be
devoured by wild beasts in the sadistic spectacles that pleased so
many Roman mobs at a coliseum. The harsh treatment of slaves
in Rome is well known. At the time of Christ, Augustus, for
example, sentenced a slave to death for having stolen and eaten
a quail. Videus Pollio amused his guests by throwing slaves to
flesh-eating fish that swam in his private pool. Sick and old
slaves sometimes exposed on an island in the Tiber River
— to die of hunger. After the time of Nero, Roman law gradually
became more humane for the slave. Under Hadrian, the whole
character of slavery was changed, wherein masters were denied
the right to kill their slaves or to treat them with excessive
brutality. They could no longer sell their slaves for their
gladiatorial combats. One must wonder what the slave would
have thought about the fourth century A.D. statement of Tyrius
Maximus: "No one is a slave whose will is free." The influence
of Christianity changed classical slavery and further restricted its
scope. The church eventually outlawed crucifixion of slaves
because the act was considered to be an ugly mirror of Christ's
death. Other inhumane treatments continued, however. For
example, if a mistress had sexual intercourse with her male
slave, the woman might be put to death and the slave burned

alive. Nevertheless, from its beginning the Christian Church emphasized that slavery was morally wrong. Despite some of St. Paul's scattered references to slavery, the teachings of Jesus were incompatible with slavery.

Between the time of Justinian and the Renaissance, European slavery came to a slow death. It can be argued that Thomas Aquinas defended slavery. Certainly St. Thomas More in his *Utopia* suggested that slaves should do "all base business and laboursome toil". In late-sixteenth-century France, Jean Bodin suggested that slavery had become extinct as early as the twelfth century. He indicated that from that time slaves could become free merely by touching French soil. (The word "slave", incidentally, originated in eighth-century France — a time when many princes were glutted with Slavonian workers.)

The Equation

Perhaps as early as 1444, some African slaves were brought to Portugal where they became agricultural labourers. A hundred years later, Blacks outnumbered Whites in Lisbon. That new form of slavery (linked to the American plantations) was arising on a greater scale than its predecessors. It is important to note that the connection between blackness and slavery is rather a recent one.

At the beginning of English settlement in the Americas, no one had intended to establish the genocidal handiwork called black slavery. Yet by the time of the American Revolution, every English mainland colony had slaves. The "peculiar institution" lasted 180 years in the Northern colonies and nearly 240 years in the South.

In Canada the statistics are no less interesting. In 1833 slavery was abolished in the British Empire. In the 370 years since the 1608 establishment of Quebec City, Canada experienced black slavery for 225 of those years — roughly sixty percent of that time period. It can be argued that slavery in New France was of the benevolent type — compared to that which was practised in the United States. In Canada slaves were bought and sold internally but there was very little international market. In other words, there was little slave trade between Canada and Africa. Nevertheless, Canada did benefit from what John Wesley termed "that execrable sum of all villainies commonly called the slave trade". In any case, Blacks came to Canada prior to the beginning of American slavery.

The first known black man to reach America was Pedro Alonso Nino who sailed with Columbus in 1492. Blacks accompanied Balboa, Ponce de Leon, Cortez, Pizarro, and Menendes. With these early white explorers and colonists came racial attitudes that existed long before the "Dutch Manne of Warre" in 1619 traded some twenty Africans for food at Jamestown, Virginia. That small group, which brought the seeds of genius and later sorrow, was only the first of between fifteen and twenty million people stolen from their African homelands. Up to sixty percent of them died during or soon after their voyage to America.

Probably North America's first legal step which linked blackness and slavery was a 1663 Maryland law which provided that all "Negroes and other slaves" within the province would have to serve for the term of their lives. In a 1681 Maryland law one paragraph included the following terms: Christian, free, English, and White. Its meaning was even more significant than is the modern, racist cliché, "free, white and twenty-one."

Slavery, most often a paying proposition, ripped the psychic identity of its victims. Docility, obedience, and service were demanded on the pain of death, brutal treatment and family separation. In spite of the Blacks' diverse backgrounds, languages, beliefs and laws, they were treated largely as one entity. The result was cultural genocide.

White on Black

Initial English contact with West Africans was not within the context of the slave trade. Blacks were simply different if "backward" people whose colour was their most arresting characteristic. In English "black" was loaded with intense and negative meanings. Long before slavery existed in America Whites associated the word with things foul, dirty, deadly, sinister, repulsive and disgraceful. The list was (and is) long. Angels were white; the Devil was black. White magic was not as terrible as black magic. The black-is-evil and white-is-pure habit of thinking was, and is, fundamental to white racism. As

14

George Best, geographer-explorer, suggested after his 1578 African voyage, black colour was a "natural infection" which set the African apart. Blacks could not possibly have the "fine attributes" of Whites.

One of the first to emphasize the gradation among human groups on the basis of physical distinctions was a mid-seventeenth century founder of the prestigious Royal Society, Sir William Petty, who stressed the physical difference found in Blacks' hair, lips, noses, and bones. He noted that Blacks differed in their "naturall manners" and in the "internall qualities" of their minds.

Another of the Society's members, surgeon Charles White, catalogued the ways in which Blacks resembled apes. Examination of Blacks' skull capacity, length of arms and legs, body odour, earlier maturation and shorter life span informed White that Africans were definitely inferior to Whites. He suggested that Blacks, perhaps like some animals, had better hearing, sense of smell, and surprisingly, a better memory.

The white intelligentsia was serious about any physical, emotional, sexual and intellectual differences between Whites and Blacks. White colonists in America most certainly shared such ideas, however vague or clear they might now appear. It is clear that even before there was slavery in Canada and the United States many Whites felt they had a "natural" superiority over Blacks. For example, the eighteenth century Scottish philosopher, David Hume, believed "Negroes to be naturally inferior to whites".

Those Whites looked to the Bible for supposed proof of their "superiority" over Blacks. Genesis 9 and 10 noted that after the great flood Noah cursed Canaan, son of Ham (whose skin was believed to be black), because the latter had looked upon his father's nakedness. Noah said Canaan must be "servant of servants". In any case, Whites believed that God's curse added to the claim that those people "scorched by the sun" were fit objects for slavery. Among other Biblical references the Book of Jeremiah (13:23) made what was considered an unfavourable comment on black skin: "Can the Ethiopian change his skin or the leopard his spots?" Many Whites believed that the Bible condoned slavery and nowhere opposed it. Many white Christians believed that Blacks were naturally the "hewers of wood and drawers of water".

Because Africans were often considered to be bestial and brutish, Whites strengthened their belief that slave traders necessarily had to handle their "black ivory" as they would beasts to be herded, branded, purchased, sold and killed when required. Africans were beastlike men just as there were man-like beasts. By such queer logic the lustful, venerous, and libidinous Blacks were thought to have excessive sexual appetites. A few Whites even chose to believe that Blacks were products of some unholy wedlock to apes. Canadian journalists of the late nineteenth century only continued the fiction. For example, as late as 1879, a Winnipeg newspaper item told of a gentle, harmless gorilla that had "the droll, quiet manners of a little black child". That equation between Blacks and gorillas was hardly unique.

Another example of Africans not living up to English standards of conduct was black heathenism. (Many slaves were raised as Muslims in their African homes.) Christianity was considered an important facet of English patriotism; it became one's duty "to change the heathen" who, after all, were "savages". Slavery was, of course, often considered a commendable method of changing the savages into Christians. Such twisted thinking unsuccessfully but conveniently covered up the real reason for the slave trade — greed.

THE CANADIAN EXAMPLE

Sticks and Stones

Black slavery arrived in what is now Canada shortly after it was introduced to North America. In 1628, nine years after a "Dutch manne of Warre" had traded slaves for food at Jamestown, Virginia, a black slave from Madagascar was sold in Montreal. His original name was discarded in favour of "Olivier Le Jeune" after his teacher, Paul Le Jeune, a Jesuit missionary.

By a series of French laws slavery was given legal foundation in New France. The 1685 "Code Noir" which regulated the practice of slavery in the West Indies, was assumed to have legal application in France's North American colony. The code was designed to protect owners from slaves' violence and escape. Outrageous cruelties were visited upon truant slaves in the name of justice. In Montreal in 1734 a black woman named Angelique, angered at the threat of being sold, set fire to her owner's house

17

whereupon she was arrested, tried, convicted, and sentenced to hang. On execution day, after being driven in a scavenger's wagon through the strets of Montreal, she was tortured and forced to "beg the king's pardon". One of her hands was then severed from its limb. Bleeding and screaming she was hanged in public view near the Place d'Armes.

The Seven Years War (1756-1763) represents the midpoint of slavery in Canada. At the time of the French Capitulation there were perhaps twelve hundred black slaves in New France. Article 47 of the 1760 Capitulation stipulated that the institution of slavery would continue under British rule. The Treaty of Paris, 1763, confirmed the plan. General James Murray, British Military Governor of Quebec and an owner of black slaves, believed slaves to be useful to the colony's economy.

That economy, unlike the plantation economies of the American South (cotton) and the West Indies (sugar), did not demand cheap labour on a large scale basis. As a result Blacks in New France served primarily as domestics, most of them being held in urban areas such as Montreal, Trois Rivières, and Quebec City.

By the mid-eighteenth century black slavery had permeated Canadian society, a society that unquestioningly sanctioned the trading off of Blacks as commodities. A Nova Scotia example indicates the attitude:

> To be sold at public auction on Monday, the 3rd of November at the house of Mr. John Rider, two slaves, viz., a boy and girl, about 11 years old likewise a puncheon of choice cherry brandy and sundry other articles.

Halifax Gazette, May 20, 1752

Similar examples are found in the newspapers of Upper Canada, Lower Canada, New Brunswick, and Prince Edward Island.

Although Canadian slaves were, by and large, better treated than their counterparts in other areas of the continent, they too found themselves at the end of the whip's lash. Near Bath, Upper Canada, a black slave was tied to a tree and whipped. In St. John's, Newfoundland a public executioner was hired to whip a Black before assembled townspeople.

Black misdemeanours demanded swift and severe responses. In 1779 two black women, accused of theft, each received twenty-five lashes at a public whipping pole in Halifax. In 1791 a Cape Breton Black was killed by a white man while attempting to enter an all-white public hall. His murderer was "honourably acquitted" but "excluded for killing a slave" from the local Masonic Lodge.

At one time slaves escaped from Canada to the United States; between 1788 and 1792 Maritime Blacks fled to the then slave-free northern states on a south-bound "underground railroad".

In 1793 Britain gave legal protection to slavery by an Imperial act that permitted the entry into Canada of "Negroes, household furniture, utensils of husbandry or clothing". To some United Empire Loyalists who had already brought their slaves with them to Canada the act must have seemed little more than formal recognition of an established practice.

In 1833 slavery was abolished within the British Empire. The enslavement of Blacks in Canada ended. Their history of second-class citizenship began.

A Cloud Upon the Future

While they were slaves Blacks in Canada posed no threat to the dominant, white society. They were without rights; they could not vote; they could not associate with white people as equals; they could not think of interracial marriage. After they were emancipated, however, the mere fact that they were no longer a people in bondage disturbed many white Canadians who now saw Blacks as a danger. Attempting to defend themselves from this new "menace", and believing that attack was, perhaps, the best defense, many prominent Canadians attacked viciously.

In 1846 Sir Richard Henry Bonnycastle described the "lower class" of Canadian Blacks as idle, impudent, uneducated people who could not "bear a little freedom". In 1859 Victoria's newspaper, *The Colonist*, claimed that the black man enjoyed fervid heat because of his "hide thicker than a hippopotamus," adding in 1860 that "Negroes are aliens of the lowest type of humanity."

While some Canadians suggested that education might be of benefit to Blacks, others disagreed. An 1884 editorial in *The Week*, a Toronto publication, asked: "Will not the negro, when educated, become even more alive to the humiliation of his social position, and learn to brood with more bitterness?" By 1887 the paper's attitude had changed. Black enlightenment seemed a good idea: "Once he (the black man) becomes thoroughly and intelligently interested in himself he ceases to be the cloud upon the future."

Canadian Blacks received sporadic, badly financed, "separate but equal" education which emphasized "practical" subjects and concerns that would "better fit the mind" of the black student. In Ontario and Nova Scotia school segregation existed in fact and in law. White children, it was felt, should not attend classes with Blacks who were lower in the social order, who learned less quickly, and whose physical presence was objectionable.

Nor were Blacks welcome in white churches. It was preferred that they find their own way to heaven. A Victoria resident's letter to the editor indicates the white attitude of the time:

> Last Sabbath was an unusually warm day. The little chapel was crowded as usual with a "small sprinkle" of blacks generously mixed in with the whites. The Ethiopians perspired! They always do when out of place.
>
> *The Colonist*, June 15, 1859

Because of this sense of unbelonging most Blacks attended their own churches. There they could find leadership, solace, and a community of friends. Some white brethren had only contempt for the black services. Beckles Willson, who described Blacks as "a dirty, good-humoured, retrograde feature of the population," observed that they went to "extremes" in their worship.

Although Blacks' churches were often schismatic and isolated from each other, they were united in their condemnation of slavery. They also frequently combined in their support for the temperance movement. Often, in a newly formed black community the first institutions to be built were the church, the school, and the temperance hall.

The gospel of Social Darwinism labelled Blacks funloving, imitative, and "naturally" obsequious. Inequality among races became a scientific theory supported by Canadian academics as well as by Canadian magazines and newspapers. An 1893 review of *Uncle Remus* in *The Week* suggested that Remus was "true to life". In actual fact, Remus, who can hardly be described as proud or forthright, was a caricature of the black man as seen by the Canadian press.

In a 1900 issue of *The Canadian Magazine* H. S. De Lesser wrote that "the negro has no strict regard for truth," adding that indeed, to the negro "there is a sort of honour attached to a certain form of lying". In the same magazine Jerome Dowd wrote of Blacks: "The burdens of the present and the future weigh lightly upon their shoulders" and "they love all worldly amusement". Agnes C. Laut spoke of the dangers of "dilution and contamination of national blood" and warned that if "coloured" people were allowed to enter Canada Canadian women would become sacrifices on an "altar of lust".

The Ultimate Canadian Race

Britton Cooke, writing in *Maclean's Magazine* in 1911, stressed the importance of developing an "Ultimate Canadian Race" and divided Canadians into two groups: Whites and others. After displaying a photograph of a typical "nigger quarter" in the United States, Cooke referred to a black Nova Scotian settlement:

> Mothers frighten the children by pointing to this gloomy shadow across the commons which separate it from the rest of the town. It is the abode of little more than innocent shiftlessness, but such places are adapted to the breeding of vice and crime.

Obviously, the Black was not considered a part of the emerging national character. His sense of humour and predisposition made him unsuitable for Canadian cities, he could cause race problems, and he likely could not be assimilated. If assimilation were possible, he would leave a "tinge" of coloured blood in the "Ultimate Canadian Race" — "a race which should be bred from the best 'stock' that can be found in the world".

21

Cooke concluded:

> The coloured man is good natured and easy going. In
> politics he is a negligible quantity. He is liable to be
> indifferent to everything but 'the fun of the thing'.
> . . . His sense of humour, his sentimentality, his
> emotionalism and his lack of initiative and executive
> ability may perhaps be overcome by education, of
> which many of them have taken advantage.

If, like Cooke, some Canadians saw Blacks as politically "a
negligible quantity," others considered them threat enough to be
denied the franchise. In 1884 *The Week* reported that "in-
feriorities of race, though indisputable, have been ignored" the
unhappy consequence being the enfranchisement of Blacks
who, as everyone knew, were "totally devoid of the capacity for
self-government". Supporting such a point of view was C. L.
Sibley's 1919 article in *The Canadian Magazine* which suggested
that Canadians would not wish to admit Blacks as equal partners
in Confederation, and certainly would not approve of Blacks
sitting in Parliament.

Cold Welcome

If Canadians couldn't have Blacks as slaves they didn't want
them at all. Vigorous attempts were made to keep Blacks out.
The climate, it was said, was too harsh for Blacks to endure.
(Oddly enough, as slaves, they had endured it for more than
two centuries. In that less enlightened time it occurred to no one
that Blacks would be happier if sent to the tropics.) The idea that
certain parts of the world were best suited to certain races was
expressed in *Some Problems of the Empire*, a 1914 address to the
Canadian Club of Ottawa by Sir Harry Hamilton Johnston. Sir
Harry wanted to keep Canada "white". "There are other
regions," he said, "which we ought to develop purely in the
interests of the black man, mainly because he suits that climate
best". Besides, as Agnes C. Laut said, "Eskimos don't live in the
tropics so why should negroes live in Canada?"

Western Canada, in particular, had a climate totally unfit for
Blacks. According to a 1911 *Manitoba Free Press* report, "Here the
cold of winter reached intensity, and it is not regarded as

physically possible for the coloured race to thrive and prosper under conditions so foreign to its origin." In the same year the *Chautauquan* claimed that Blacks could not "endure or thrive under the rigours of the Canadian climate". And if they tried they would "degenerate, and become paupers". A. Brambley-Moore, an Albertan who thought that Blacks could better "live and breed in tropical countries," said that they constituted "a possible menace to the supremacy of the white race," and thus could be barred from Canada "under the law of self-preservation".

In 1910 George Parkin, a prominent writer, speaker, and Canadian imperialist, suggested that the nation's climate gave it a social and political advantage over the United States which had a race problem weighing "like a troublesome nightmare". He argued that climate gave Canadians a Puritan turn of mind; it would keep out undesirable races through a Darwinian process of natural selection. While emphasizing that Canada should remain colour conscious he compared Canadians favourably with Americans who "have not made impossible the oppression or abuse of inferior races, black, red or yellow". Climate, he maintained, could keep Canada white.

The transparency of the climate argument is hardly open to question. It made no difference that in 1909 Matthew Henson, a Black, was claimed to be a co-discoverer of the North Pole. Blacks simply could not endure the cold and therefore should stay out. Canada's mission and destiny demanded other stock.

The Black West

In the Canadian West, which is the focus of this book, the Black was often an object of ridicule and gutter humour. "Possum with gravy" was said to be the favourite food of Blacks while "the definition of a disgusted negro" was "a buck bored". In 1884 the humour section of the Fort Macleod newspaper related an imaginary conversation between a white judge and a wide-eyed Black accused of stealing from a clothes line:

> "I say, boss, I don't keer to put de court and de sheriff
> to trouble on my account. Jess lemme off ag'in wid a
> repriman', as you did las' week, on account ob hit
> being my fust offense, an'll plead guilty ter five

chickens I pulled las' week, an' a hog I stole las' winter, an' a pair ob shoes from de store, an' a woodpile I'se gwineter haul off to-night."

Macleod Gazette, October 17, 1884

Would Western pioneers have laughed less loudly if they had had personal experience with a black man's courage and strength? Would experience with a black man's kindness, gentleness, and warmth have altered their views about the "Ultimate Canadian"? Examination of the life and times of cowboy John Ware provides some answers.

JOHN WARE

He was our Dad, a good father and we loved him.
                              — Nettie Ware, Vulcan, Alberta

A Seventy-Year Memory

It was both beautiful and sad to see tears in the old lady's eyes. Amanda Janet "Nettie" Ware, Vulcan, Alberta's spirited octogenarian, and her province's 1971 "Pioneer Daughter", recalled the 1905 death of her father, John Ware. After seven decades his zest, kindness, love of life, and strength of body and character were lovingly remembered by Nettie, a daughter of the "big slave". Her tears came from pride and sorrow.

The "big slave", as Ware was commonly called in Alberta, was toughened for and by the frontier. The six-foot plus, 230-pound strong man with the hearty laugh became the best known Black on the early Canadian prairies. He lived a full life. He suffered. He survived where many would have succumbed. His children remember his spirit and verve, they cherish his love of family, and they dismiss what some of today's black pride advocates might call his "Uncle Tomism".

25

The allegation would be unfair. John Ware, initially shaped by slavery's whip, was partially reshaped by the Western Canadian frontier. His big frame planted firmly on Canadian soil responded to the land's demand for hard work, courage, and patience for another day. But, the cattle country could not teach him certain kinds of restraint; he often did courageous things which today seem foolhardy. That lack of restraint combined with his personal magnetism and practical mind led to his wide acceptance in a Canadian society that was not ready to receive most Blacks as equals.

Ware, a man of action rather than of introspection, at times did little in the face of outright racial prejudice. Was it patience or resignation that allowed him to accept his nickname, "Nigger John" — a term he used on himself? Was it Uncle Tomism that allowed him to dance and jig for the pleasure of white audiences? Did he display his immense physical strength more to prove something to himself than to entertain and impress the white community? If some answers appear affirmative they must be placed in the following context: perhaps more than anyone discussed in this book, Ware was a product of two widely differing environments — the Deep South and the Canadian West.

The first years of Ware's life were shaped by that most barbarous of human institutions — slavery. It is impossible to comprehend the psychic, emotional, and spiritual damage inflicted on him during these years. Perhaps the former slave always carries the shackles' scars. Ware did. To the end of his life he remained a partial prisoner of his first twenty years.

Down Home

In 1845 John Ware was born into a South Carolina slave family. In some ways his family was more fortunate than others: his parents and their ten children had not been separated. The family had a father, a situation which did not often exist in slave families. (For this reason some writers claim that black families today are matriarchal — a legacy of slavery.)

The Wares lived in their own shanty away from their master's house. Sometimes on Sundays the slaves were permitted a certain kind of recreation. An area was roped off or formed by spectators, and two black youths were forced to fight each other until one was vanquished. John Ware fought often; because of his size and strength he usually won. Such master-sponsored exhibitions were encouraged for two reasons especially: the entertainment of the spectators and release of the slaves' pent-up frustration and hatred. Throughout his life a part of John Ware remained the exhibition fighter.

Singing was another kind of release. To a degree music could overcome the spiritual brutality of slavery. Black songs often contained messages of freedom. Some clearly mocked the owner. Spirituals told of a better life to come. Meanwhile, the white church preached that the master and mistress were really God's overseers: to betray one's owners was to betray God.

In South Carolina by 1860 a "prime male" slave like Ware was worth up to $1300 — quite an investment. As a result, delinquent slaves were seldom killed by their masters. Instead, they were thrashed and mutilated. Sometimes they were branded. One day, Ware saw one of his sisters being manhandled by the master. Enraged, he knocked the man to the ground. As a punishment he was tied to a tree and whipped. He never forgot the experience. A whipping he had received as a small boy had been administered by a snake hide. As a consequence, Ware hated and feared snakes to his grave.

By 1860 there were roughly 385,000 slave owners in the South. Fewer than 3,200 owned a hundred slaves or more. In some areas the ownership of even two or three slaves guaranteed some status. Hollywood's portrayals of Southern plantations have usually included Georgian mansions served by house and field slaves. The house slaves often were only a "step above" the field slaves who, for the most part, lived in rough shanties. The movie stereotype is further diminished by the realization that a few slave owners were black.

It is unlikely that the fifteen-year-old Ware realized that by 1860 slavery was a decaying institution. The spirit of the times was against it, and much world opinion was directed against slave owners. In many Southern areas the depletion of the soil by a one-crop system was making slavery less economical. Some Southerners correctly realized that slavery could not survive the economic stress of war. (In 1865 President Davis offered to abolish slavery if Britain would recognize the Confederacy.)

Even if secession had succeeded slavery would have eventually died; slaves would have been induced to escape, abolitionists would have continued their successful propaganda, and the moral stance of the slave owners would not have withstood world public opinion. Had some Northerners been less blinded by emotion these possibilities might have received more adequate consideration.

Emotional pressures and sectional exacerbations led to the events at Fort Sumter, South Carolina — fifty miles from the Georgetown home of John Ware, his parents, and ten brothers and sisters. On April 13, 1861, after thirty-four hours of bombardment, the fort fell to the Confederate forces and war began.

The Civil War (1861-1865) was to decide whether the United States was really a nation or merely a collection of sovereign independent states. The slavery issue was not the first priority, although a slave like John Ware might have debated the point. The Blacks' miseries did not end with Lincoln's 1865 Emancipation Proclamation, or with the Thirteenth Amendment which stated that "Neither slavery nor involuntary servitude shall . . . exist within the United States." Robert E. Lee's April 9, 1865 surrender to Ulysses S. Grant at Appomattox, Virginia, and Lincoln's martyrdom signalled the beginning of the Reconstruction Era, which was simply a new chapter in the Blacks' frustrations.

After the first heady euphoria of freedom, the reality of their position changed loudly in the minds of many former slaves. The following account makes the point clearly:

> We all gathered at the "big house". A stranger read the Emancipation Proclamation. We were told that we were all free, and could go when we pleased. My mother kissed her children, while tears of joy ran down her cheeks. For some minutes there was great rejoicing, and thanksgiving, but by the time the slaves returned to their cabins there was a change in their feelings. . . . These were the questions of a home, a living, the rearing of children, education, and citizenship. . . . Gradually, one by one, stealthily at first, the older slaves began to wander from the slave quarters back to the "big house" to have

whispered conversation with their former owners as
to the future.

Many freed Blacks had no choice but to ask "Ol' Massa" for a
job. Some worked on "shares" which really only continued the
habit of much work with little or no reward. The owner supplied
materials, seed, machinery, tools, and housing; the black
sharecroppers supplied the labour. At harvest the owner often
took half the profits plus costs for the things he provided. Little
was left for the Blacks: they became, in many instances, another
kind of slave — people with little or no hope for change.

One young Black, John Ware, had had enough of sharecrop-
ping, the Ku Klux Klan, second-class citizenship, corrupt
officialdom, and hopelessness. He left South Carolina and his
family, who never saw him again, for Texas where he could find
open spaces. His confinement ended. Never again did he have
to answer the often-asked question, "Whose nigger are you?"

A Different Branding Iron

The young Ware, with South Carolina behind him, soon
found work in Texas. Near Fort Worth he began his cowboy
career on the Murphy Blandon ranch. Here he became skilled
with horses and the lariat. It was also here that he was
introduced to guns and for the rest of his life he wore a six-gun
and holster. His uncanny knowledge of horses, his sense of
humour, and his prodigious strength were valued by the
Blandon family. He proved that in the saddle colour meant
nothing. On the Blandon ranch the branding iron was reserved
for cattle.

The legend and reality of the cowboy were born after the
American Civil War. The great cattle drives from Texas
northward demanded men prepared for long, lonely months on
the trail. The objectives were clear: to survive, and to get the
cattle to market. Today's movies and television have largely
ignored the black cowboys, badmen, and sheriffs. But, in some
areas of the Southwest more than one third of the cowboys were
black. Many of them, like John Ware, were former slaves who
were usually assigned the lowliest jobs on the ranch, or served
as dragmen on the trail.

In 1882 Ware was asked to take cattle north to Montana's

markets. With other men he led 2,500 head some two thousand miles north. The drive meant four months in the saddle. One cowboy, Bill Moodie, became friendly with Ware. When the herd reached Montana the two men prospected unsuccessfully for gold. In spite of their failure they loved the more northerly region. When two cattlemen, Tom Lynch and Fred Stimson, offered them a chance to drive cattle to Alberta they gladly accepted the challenge. In September of 1882, John Ware, the thirty-seven-year-old ex-slave, entered Canada. He was never to leave his adopted land. He was free — a lone Black on a frontier that was meant to be white.

Double Rates

The cowboys drove their cattle ten to fifteen miles a day along and near the Whoop-Up Trail which connected Fort Benton, Montana to Fort Whoop-Up (Lethbridge). On their way north to "The Crossing" (near Calgary) the men stopped at Fort Macleod, then headquarters of the North-West Mounted Police. There, on a wall of the hotel owned by Harry "Kamoose" Taylor, was a notice that has become famous in Western Canada. It was intended to be humourous, exaggerating as it did the rough spirit of the early Canadian West. One item on the poster speaks volumes: "Indians and niggars charged double rates."

One "nigger", John Ware, often paid "double rates" during his life on the Canadian range land. As often as not he had to work twice as hard and twice as long as a white man in order to achieve the same kind of acceptance. The "double rates" he paid were not only those demanded by the likes of "Kamoose" Taylor. Most of the demands on him came from inside. He was driven, a man whose earlier slave experience forced him to almost superhuman effort to accomplish and to be loved. As a slave he had been psychologically shackled; as an Alberta cowboy he gloried in the wide open spaces.

In 1883 the spring round-up sent Ware and other cattlemen between the Highwood and Old Man rivers. Near Fort Macleod they were asked to break an untamed horse called Mustard. After others had been thrown to the ground in the attempt, Ware mounted the horse which raced toward the Old Man

River's steep cliffs. Horse and rider sailed through the air landing squarely in the cold water. Ware stayed in the saddle and rode Mustard out of the river to meet the admiring cowboys. He was becoming more than a black curiosity: his daring and courage had won him respect as a man.

Ware's escapades drew the attention of the *Macleod Gazette*, Alberta's pioneer newspaper. In 1885 its editor interviewed Ware after he had survived another watery plunge, this one almost taking his life. During a river crossing Ware's horse panicked, heaving its rider into the water. Encumbered by his heavy, water-soaked slicker, chaps and clothes, Ware struggled until thrown a rope by which he was able to pull himself to shore. He described the experience:

> Would you believe it, but I'll be dog-garned if those fellers didn't stand on the shore and laugh at me, an' me just drownin' all the time. When I struck bottom an' got out on the bank I looked as if I'd been drowned about two months an' was just resurrected. Them fellers, they just stood an' laughed, an' one of 'em says: "Git wet, John?" . . . Them fellers must have knowed I was wet, slicker and all, 'cause I looked like a drowned rat.
>
> *Macleod Gazette*, June 23, 1885

Ware obviously enjoyed telling the story. He concluded: "I'll tell you . . . they're a great lot of boys, an' full of the devil, you bet!" The big slave was home on the range.

The vision of instant wealth had not quite left Ware. With Prince Edward Island-born Dan Riley (later Senator Riley) and frontiersman Lafayette French he rode west to the Crowsnest Pass region in search of the legendary Lost Lemon Mine which was thought to be in the Livingston Range near the source of the Old Man and Highwood rivers. The men knew of the mine's curse. In the 1870s, according to the story, Lemon murdered his partner after they had found riches in gold. After marking the mine's location Lemon returned to his Montana home. The ghost of his victim, Black Jack, followed him, causing Lemon to lose his sanity. On repeated returns to the area of the mine his attempts to claim the gold were thwarted by Black Jack's ghost. Others who sought the gold died mysteriously or disappeared.

Ware, a superstitious man, did not discount the legend. He was happy to return empty-handed to the Crossing.

In 1884 Ware made his first trip to Calgary. Unaware of a recent murder committed by Jesse Williams, another Black, he was hurt when told to leave town. Popular sentiment seemed to be that all Blacks were guilty of one Black's crime.

Like many cattlemen, Ware disliked sheep. The *Calgary Herald* reported that 8,000 sheep crossed the Bow River and were "fat as butter". The whole idea disgusted Ware: "Sheep just eat too close to the ground and will spoil the grassland for cattle." He would have agreed with Fort Macleod's Stock Association whose 1884 petition to Ottawa demanded that "sheep be not allowed to graze on the open prairie south of Sheep Creek".

Ware disliked sheep, but he despised wolves and coyotes. He was delighted when either fell to his revolver or rifle. His daughter, Nettie, remembers the day in 1905 when from his kitchen door he shot a coyote which had come too near the ranch house. His dislike of wolves was understandable. In one year twenty-four cattle from his herd were killed by the predators.

To combat the wolf and coyote problem a number of the larger cattle ranchers kept hunting-hounds. The Cochrane ranch hounds separately killed nearly ten dozen coyotes in one 1889 month. It was not uncommon for ranchers to combine their hounds and go on a coyote-wolf drive. Often several hundred animals were killed on one Sunday "outing". Sport may have played as large a part as necessity in the coyote-wolf hunt, for the fox hunt was popular as well:

> Lethbridge has gone wild over fox hunting. A number had been captured and on this particular Sunday the town turned out almost en masse to give chase. As many as could get anything in the shape of an animal with four legs were mounted. Having arrived at the spot the foxes were let out one by one and the pack of hounds, from fox terriers to Newfoundland, let loose. Then the fun began. Another fox turned toward town and arrived, followed by a wildly enthusiastic crowd, both mounted and driving, just as the children were going to Sunday School. The fever seized the latter. The fox

darted across the railway track and the children joined pell mell in pursuit. Religiously inclined people felt much shocked.

Macleod Gazette, October 5, 1889

Whether or not Ware approved of hunting as a sport, he did enjoy sports that called for one-on-one skill and endeavour. He may have been the first man in Western Canada to earn the title of "steer wrestler". In 1892, when he wrestled a huge, rampaging Walrond ranch steer to the ground, the cowboys on the Old Man River's bank cheered his strength and skill. Ware's action had been one of desperation: the steer had charged him. In subsequent years he performed publicly, in 1893 winning an expensive saddle for his exploits.

Calgarians continued the roping and wrestling competitions. The spirit of the now famous Calgary Stampede was born. Ware entered the 1894 competition only to disappoint the gamblers who bet on him.

The roping contest at the Calgary exhibition this summer was a very poor affair, from the western point of view, although it probably delighted those who had never seen it before. John Weir who roped and tied his steer last year in something like 58 sec. started out with every prospect of lowering his own record. The steer had not made half a dozen jumps before John turned him over. He had tied him in no time, but in his anxiety to make time, did the work carelessly, and before the time limit, five minutes, expired, the steer had kicked himself clear and got onto his feet. There was great disappointment among the crowd, John having been backed pretty heavily to win.

Macleod Gazette, July 27, 1894

Many accounts credit another black cowboy, Will Pickett, billed as the "Dusky Demon", with being the first bulldogger in Western Canada. Pickett, who travelled the rodeo circuit, performed his feat in 1905 before the Calgary exhibition grandstand. He was managed by young Guy Weadick, who later toured with Buffalo Bill Cody. Some consider the romantic Weadick the originator of the Calgary Stampede. Perhaps Weadick deserves the compliment; perhaps John Ware's name should replace Will Pickett's.

Ware was a born horseman and a superb rider, probably the best throughout Alberta cow country. Ranchers called on him to break wild horses, and he responded with enthusiasm. He was proud of his ability and loved to display it. It was the Sunday exhibition fight of his youth all over again.

News of John Ware's skill with horses spread far and wide. On one occasion, after he had been out on a spree in Calgary and arrested for drunkenness, he was brought before a magistrate who recognized him as the famous black bronc-buster. It so happened that the judge had a horse in need of taming, and John Ware was just the man to do the job. Case dismissed! The occasional taste of city life was quite enough for Ware. He had come to love the prairie, and the prairie had, in its own way, made a place for him.

The 1885 Threat

By the time of Ware's arrival on the prairie in 1882, the great buffalo herds had largely vanished. The Indians had, in the previous decade, surrendered most of their lands through treaties and were now confined to reservations. The advance of white settlement brought an abrupt end to the buffalo hunt and the Indians' old way of life. By the mid-1880s they faced starvation. Indians near Ware's High River home were desperate as a report from Ware's friend, Fred S. Stimson, manager of the Northwest Cattle Company, indicated:

> There were three bucks, three squaws and half a dozen children and the whole of them were actually gaunt with famine. One of the young bucks, naturally a strong, hearty lad, had an arm no thicker than my wrist. . . . Well, I gave them something to eat, not roasts especially, because they might get too fat, but parts that white men don't usually eat, and the Indians just warmed the meat by the fire and bolted it whole.
>
> *Calgary Herald*, February 12, 1885

Stimson's report, condescending and abusive, indicated the prevailing attitude toward Indians. And men like Ware had added to the problem of starvation through thoughtless over-hunting of the foothills and grass country. Red anger flared. In Saskatchewan, Indians and Métis rose up under Dumont, Big Bear, Poundmaker, and Riel. The 1885 North-West Rebellion had broken out.

Most of the North-West Mounted Police were called into Saskatchewan, leaving the white settlements in Alberta with little protection and facing the threat of a general Indian uprising. As a result several home guards were formed. John Ware joined one of them, Stimson's Rangers. The Indians knew him as Metoxy Sex Apee Quin — Bad Black White Man. He had a stake in Alberta's future and was ready to fight. As it turned out, the rebellion was short-lived; Big Bear, Poundmaker, and Riel had all been captured by July 2, little more than three months after the first clash at Duck Lake on March 26.

More usually, the N.W.M.P. had its hands full in its attempts to rid the West of vile bootleg whiskey. One frontier recipe called for "equal quantities of Canadian pain destroyer and yellow oil and a bottle of each poured together and half the mess taken at one draught". No name for the drink had been coined, the English language having been "not sufficiently expressive".

Clothes Make the Man?

> If the average cowboy has any love for the beautiful at all, it is for his silver-mounted horse-rig, his gaudy sash and tassels.
>
> *Macleod Gazette,* August 14, 1882

Ware liked gaudy clothes if and when he could acquire them. On special occasions he wore a fancy Prince Albert coat, a gift he received in 1886 from a visiting English lord — a man who had come to hunt the vanished buffalo. (Ware was usually impressed by titles and "important" people.)

Family Man

By 1890 Ware had his own ranch on the Sheep Creek, near Calgary. His cattle, branded with four nines (9999), brought him a handsome profit. (Some people incorrectly believe that Ware thought nine to be his lucky number because, it has been said, he was nine years old when emancipated. In actual fact, he was twenty years old at the time.) More than anything he wanted to share the future with a wife. It is probable that he never would have considered an interracial marriage.

In the same year he learned that a young black girl, Mildred Lewis, had arrived with her family, Mr. and Mrs. Daniel V. Lewis, in the Calgary area. Ware wasted no time in seeking them out. They met in Calgary. The Lewis family was impressed by Ware and it is likely that the nineteen-year-old Mildred found him attractive — he was a striking figure with his spade-shaped beard and Prince Albert coat.

In the best tradition of late-Victorian courtesy Mrs. Lewis invited Ware for Sunday supper. The inspired cowboy rode twenty-five miles from his ranch to the new Lewis homestead at Shephard to accept her hospitality. It scarcely mattered to him that he had to ride across the Bow River. He knew what he wanted. He had waited a long time for an opportunity like this.

Not many courting couples have had an experience similar to one of John's and Mildred's. On a July day in 1890 the couple went for a buggy ride with some friends. The day which had begun beautifully was interrupted by an angry summer storm. A lightning bolt struck the horses, knocking them to the ground but the passengers were not hurt. (Eight decades later daughter Nettie insisted that her father had saved Mildred and friends by throwing a rubber slicker over them.) One wonders if the superstitious Ware interpreted the incident as a good or bad omen. In any case, he left the horses where they had fallen and pulled the buggy and passengers home by himself. "Yes," said Nettie, "he was a man who made the best of whatever a situation might be."

On Christmas Day, 1891, he proposed. On Leap Year Day (February 29, 1892) they were married in Calgary's Baptist Church. Their return to the ranch house was welcomed by a frontier-style chivaree. It was a happy time for John Ware.

The marriage gave the Wares five children: Amanda (Nettie), Robert, twins William and Mildred, and Arthur. A sixth child, Daniel, died in infancy. Nettie recalled that her father was "a jovial man but still his word was his bond, and if he promised anybody anything that was it". If one of the boys misbehaved father John would pick him up with one hand, shake him, place him on his own broad shoulders and carry him to the house. Nettie remembers "being taken out to the woodshed when I was bad. Yes," she said, "we were made to mind."

Father John "was not a regular church-goer," Nettie added, but "my mother came from a religious family and when we were kids we had to get down and say our prayers every night, regular as night come". Mother Mildred read the Bible aloud to her family and taught the children their first Sunday school lessons.

Not until after the children were born did Ware learn to sign his name. He was a proud man and in his opinion a good father had to be a good example to his children; he learned to write. Mildred would place her hand over his and guide the pencil over the paper. In the evenings she read to him from the *Calgary Herald* and from farm publications.

By 1900 John Ware and his family had moved from the "crowded" foothills area of Sheep Creek to the more remote Millarville near present-day Brooks. Nettie recalled the long wagon journey through Calgary east to the new homestead: "It was an exciting trip but our Dad knew about things so we weren't afraid." The children slept under the wagon. The parents slept in it.

Ware's destination was a site near the Red Deer River where "the grass was shorter but sweeter". There he built a small cabin on a creek bank. Nettie remembers happy times: Saturday night parades to the wooden bathtub, Sunday democrat rides to new picnic places, first school lessons taught by Mother, visits to Grandma Lewis in Calgary, and visits by new friends and neighbours.

Ware briefly considered joining the Klondike gold rush, 1898, and the Boer War, 1899-1902, but selling horses that served in the South African conflict was a close as he came to either. There was challenge enough on the prairies.

Nature provided challenge. The creek's wet cold anger wiped out the Wares' cabin. With friends' help the family rebuilt on higher ground. Further difficulty came from mange, a disease of cattle. Ware promptly built a dipping pit where cattle were washed with a chemical solution. The jovial Ware was the first to laugh when he himself fell head first into the pit.

Mildred enjoyed occasional visits with her parents who had moved to Blairmore, a gateway to the Crow's Nest Pass, and only a few miles from where her husband had earlier searched for the Lost Lemon Mine. On one of those visits Mildred and Nettie narrowly escaped death; the Frank Slide disaster struck while they were in "The Pass". At 4:10 a.m., April 29, 1903, more than 72,000,000 tons of Turtle Mountain's rock crashed down onto the sleeping settlement of Frank, leaving sixty-six of its citizens buried to this day. Nettie Ware recalled the awful morning clearly:

> It had turned dark and cold. Oh my, it had turned cold. Everyone was screaming and running. Our window looked towards Frank and we thought there must have been a disaster at the mine. When Mother and I found out about those poor people we cried for a long, long time.

Over the years John and Mildred met few people of their own colour. One of Blairmore's few Blacks, Pete Smith, cooked and did chores for Mildred's parents. A black cowboy, Leige Abel, had worked for the Walrond ranch, and another ex-slave worked for rancher Tony Day. Black travellers occasionally passed through Calgary and Lethbridge.

Most prairie people who knew Ware treated him fairly and openly. Strangers were often less receptive to his black face. In Medicine Hat, for example, he was refused accomodation in a hotel until friends "set the hotel man straight". In the same town a white man threw a dead snake at Ware, who responded by throwing the man across the street. In Calgary where he was the target of a drunk's racial barbs Ware knocked the man senseless and then took him to a hospital and paid the doctor's bill. However, such action was not typical of Ware: more often than not he walked away from a real fight. He was no crusader and he made no quixotic attempts to rid his adopted prairies of prejudice. He did not even think in those terms: his life included his family, work, and friends.

Sadness

In the spring of 1905 Ware's mother-in-law visited the ranch house. At breakfast she told him of a dream she had had during the night: "John, you are going to get your hasty news." "Mother Ware", as John called her, continued: "Whenever I

38

dream of fire and see flames, it means hasty news, and last night I dreamed that way." Before breakfast was finished a rider appeared with bad news. Mildred, ill with fever in a Calgary hospital, had died. John was crushed; he had waited so many years for someone like Mildred and now she was gone.

Ware rode to Battery (Brooks) and caught the westbound train to Calgary. Nettie and other of the children, who were staying with their grandfather at Blairmore, took the train to Calgary by way of Fort Macleod. Seventy years later she remembered the trip:

> It was a sad time and we cried on the train. There was the awfulest stop-over in Macleod. Mother was gone and we sure loved her.

Mrs. Lewis, John, and the children returned to the ranch. Pete Smith, their black friend from Blairmore, accompanied the sorrowing family. Nettie reminisced:

> Old Pete Smith was no good to himself when he could get liquor but he helped us just the same. Father couldn't have had a better man because he could cook, he could mend clothes, and he could mend fences.

The summer of 1905 came and its work helped to fill Ware's emptiness. It was forty years since he had been a slave, and twenty-three years since he had crossed the Canadian border. At sixty he was still a commanding figure. Before his wife's death he could have looked forward to a bright future in Alberta.

Ware knew little of the political forces that were leading Alberta and Saskatchewan into Confederation. He knew nothing of another lone prairie Black, Alfred Schmitz Shadd, who, in those summer months, spoke to other settlers, convincing them that prairie folk must demand their rights within the bounds of Confederation. Ware was not a political animal; his world was one of sweat and callouses and now sorrow.

Ware's West had changed. He saw the last of the buffalo, perhaps the first of the automobiles. By 1905 one could "speed" by train from Winnipeg to Edmonton in twenty-seven hours.

Twenty years earlier he had ridden guard against the Riel-related Indian threat. Now the political issues were Confederation, wheat prices, freight rates and immigration. As he rode near Nigger John Coulee and Nigger John Creek (later so-named in his "honour") he must have said to himself: "I have come a long way from slavery."

But had he? The Calgary newspaper that Mildred had read to him on quiet nights called "a curious proposition" the suggestion of one black writer that "the two races experience amalgamation". Black men were still being hanged in his native United States for looking at or flirting with white females. The Ku Klux Klan, which would come to the prairies thirty years later, was still using bed sheets and fiery crosses to cover warped hatred. In many ways, Ware, as a lone Black, was "a curious proposition" to many Whites: he was humorous, enormously strong, dependable, helpful, and — harmless. He was no threat to the settlers' demand for racial "purity".

It was as if Ware's huge frame could withstand most hurts, physical and psychological. Perhaps slavery's scar tissue was thick enough to protect him from whatever life in Canada could offer. It is equally likely that his ignorance of the magnitude of prairie prejudice allowed him his own brand of happiness.

Here was a man who had survived slavery's hell, cattle stampedes, harsh climate, and years of hard work. On September 12, 1905, as he was riding near his ranch, his horse stepped into a badger's hole and fell heavily to the ground. The saddle horn that had known Ware's hands a thousand times found his chest. He died instantly. His dog stayed by the body until help came.

His death was announced the same day:

JOHN WARE KILLED

Well Known Colored Ranger Meets
Sudden Death

Brooks, N.W.T. Sept. 12 — John Ware, commonly called "Nigger John", and ex-slave from the south and for twenty-five a rancher and cowhand in the west, owner of a thousand head of finest range cattle on the Red Deer River, was killed today by a horse stumbling and falling upon him, killing him instantly.

Deceased was 60 years old and leaves a family. Ware was one of the most widely known ranchers in this district. He was famous as a roper and rider, and always won first money in any of the competitions he entered. He was a man of prodigious strength, and with apparent ease he could pick up an 18-months old steer and throw him ready for branding. Any person who has tried to throw a six-months old steer will realize that this feat is no small one. Ware first came to Canada with Fred Stimson and the Bar U cattle. He was with them for some years, then was foreman of the large Macpherson horse ranche and later on of the Quorn ranche on Sheep Creek. He started for himself on Sheep creek and ran a ranche there for nine years, removing to the Red Deer, where he has since lived. His wife died this spring.

The Daily Herald, Calgary, September 12, 1905

Young Nettie, son Bob, Pete Smith, and an old friend, John Eide, hitched up the buck board and took the body to Brooks, then no more than a whistle stop. The dead man was taken by railroad to Calgary.

Today's Alberta was one week old when Ware died. He would have been pleased that by the above technically incorrect announcement he was identified with the Northwest Territories. After all, the Territories represented his time, space, and way of life. After a large Baptist church funeral attended by many friends, he was buried beside Mildred.

Ware would have laughed loudly if he could have known what happened to an old friend, Sam Howe, who unsuccessfully attempted to go the funeral. Sam had heard about the accident while working at a ranch on the Belly River. After riding to Lethbridge he learned that in order to get to the Calgary funeral on time he would have to travel by train to Medicine Hat and then switch to another going to Calgary. After telling the conductor that he was going "to John's funeral" Sam fell asleep. When he awoke he found that he was just outside Swift Current, Saskatchewan. He made it to Calgary a day late. In tribute to his friend Sam got roaring drunk.

Five years later Ware's brother, George, was interviewed by a reporter for the *Edmonton Daily Bulletin.* The news item, titled

"Former Slave Asks for Job in Calgary," referred to George Ware as "an 80-year old veritable Uncle Tom". Apparently, in 1865 he left the Deep South to make his way to the Chatham area of Kent County, Ontario. The report added that he had come to Calgary when his brother, John, was killed.

The item offers at least two significant thoughts for consideration: members of John's family knew about his life in Alberta, and John's 1882 move to Canada may have been prompted by George's earlier action.

George Ware who "knew nothing but toil and abuse from his brutal overseers," told the reporter how he lost the use of one eye:

> Chile, ah lost ma poor ole eye w'en ah was a kiddy workin' on de ole plantation . . . dat ole black mammy who was alookin' after us hit me in mah eye wit' a peach tree switch, an' ah ain't nevvah had much use o' it since.
>
> *Edmonton Daily Bulletin*, June 20, 1910

The old man who had "lost most of the wool from the top of his head," who complained about sore feet, and who carried a stout walking stick was represented as another object of curiosity. "Uncle George", as he was called by the reporter, had asked the city's mayor for "a little something to do so that he might live". In spite of his perhaps unfair Uncle Tom image, the old gentleman was true to the Ware name: he wanted work, not charity.

The Lewis family raised the Ware children to serve God and the world. As Nettie said: "Grandma taught us learning and Grandpa taught us praying." The children began to hear tales of John Ware, the legend: John Ware once bent an iron survey peg to make a splint for a man's broken shoulder; to bring medicine for his wife, John Ware once walked twenty-five miles from Brooks to his ranch through a blinding snowstorm; when "Nigger John" first came to these parts he threw a match on a pond and it burned — it was really John Ware who discovered the Turner Valley gas fields; "Jolly John" surely could dance, jig, and sing to the music of the fiddle; John Ware was the toughest man in the saddle these parts have ever seen and the N.W.M.P. at Ford Macleod gave him the most ornery broncos to break;

John Ware once held two frightened horses by their necks as a train roared past them.

Some of the stories grew with the telling. Others simply indicated that Ware was a unique man in a difficult time and place. His name is attached to a coulee, a creek, a museum, and a Calgary school. In short, he was one of the most remarkable people on the Western Canadian frontier.

Nettie Ware, perhaps the first black child born in the Northwest Territories, does not think of her father as an ex-slave, or as an object for study. "No," she said simply, "he was our Dad, a good father and we loved him."

DOC SHADD

The spring of 1896 gave sweet promise to the scattered homesteaders of the Carrot River Valley. J.M. (Silvertip) Campbell drove the Prince Albert mail wagon through the near-virginal park land to Kinistino in Canada's Northwest Territories. Passenger Alfred Schmitz Shadd, a black man, must have wondered if he could belong to that frontier time and place.

The twenty-six-year-old Shadd was a shock to some Kinistino children who had never seen a black man; he was to be their teacher. After arranging for a room and board at the home of Charlie Lowrie, the local postmaster, Shadd took his books and supplies to the Agricultural Hall — the cultural, religious, and educational centre of the settlement. When class was not in session Shadd's schoolroom echoed with dance, music, and laughter, witnessed God's children worshipping, and listened to homesteaders' talk of wheat prices, railroads, hunting, immigration, and economic survival.

The young educator was to cut a wide swath in the Carrot River Valley's farming communities. For nearly twenty years he was to equal and often surpass in hard work the neighbouring farmers, storekeepers, and lumbermen. His energy, humour, intelligence, and humanity were to be useful to and admired by the settlers.

Shadd, the fourth son of Garrison and Harriet Poindexter Shadd, was born in 1870 on his father's farm on the Seventh Concession, Raleigh Township, Kent County, Ontario. He came from a family of consistent accomplishment. Many of his forefathers were activists who strove to achieve social equality for Canadian Blacks. His grandfather, Abraham Doras Shadd (1801-1882), came to Raleigh County, Ontario (Canada West) after the passage of the 1850 American Fugitive Slave Bill. In 1853 Abraham's family and his brother, Absalom, moved from Wilmington, Delaware to Westchester, Pennsylvania. After his arrival in Canada, Abraham and family worked to rid their adopted country of racism. Josiah Henson, often erroneously referred to as the original and only "Uncle Tom" in Harriet Beecher Stowe's famous book, was aided by Abraham. (When Alfred was thirteen years old, Chatham, Ontario's all-black band attended the 1883 funeral of the ninety-three-year-old "Uncle Tom" who was buried in the nearby community of Dresden.) Abraham probably also collaborated with William Lloyd Garrison, the American abolitionist. In 1859 Abraham became the first Black to be elected to a public office (Raleigh Town Council) in Canada West. With black brethren he established Masonic lodges throughout that part of Canada.

Abraham's children were no less active. Mary Anne and Isaac were editors; Emmaline and Eunice became teachers; Elizabeth was a circuit rider; Garrison was a successful farmer; and Abraham Jr. was admitted to the Mississippi bar.

Perhaps Mary Anne was the most remarkable member of Abraham Shadd's family. She was a Quaker-educated teacher, who, as editor of the (Canada West) *Provincial Freeman*, strongly opposed Henry Bibbs' newspaper, *Voice of the Fugitive*, which, she felt, considered Canada only a temporary stopping place for Blacks who had arrived by the famous but overestimated ı "Underground Railway". Canada, she believed, should be a permanent home for black people. She demanded equality for Blacks while scorning white racism and black acquiescence. This honest and vigorous woman, who left institutionalized religion because of her well-founded belief that some churches supported racial segregation, became a major voice among the Blacks of Canada West.

By the mid-1850s nearly 1,600 Blacks or twenty-five per cent of the area's black population lived in Chatham. (It seems likely that the 1861 estimate of 60,000 Blacks in Canada West was an exaggerated total.) Shadd's Chatham gained a reputation as a tough town for Blacks. Black citizens tended to be more urbanized than other groups, this feature making them more visible and threatening. (Historically, Canadian Blacks have tended to live in clusters as appendages to white settlements. Chicken coops and laundry lines were once thought to be temptations too strong for many Blacks to resist.) Hotels and many public places were banned to Blacks. In the 1890s one Chatham barber won local fame by refusing service to a black man because no black soap was available. As late as 1908, a Chatham Black received forty lashes and a five-year jail sentence for "luring a white girl from her home". The incident was only one of many which indicated the Canadian taboo on interracial sexual relations.

Racially segregated schools existed by law (the 1850 legislation remained until 1964), and residential segregation existed because it was expected. Gerrymandering of school district boundaries helped to keep black and white children apart. However, the courts were slowly killing the segregated school idea — an 1861 case in Shadd's town was an example. In Simmons Vs. Chatham Chief Justice John Beverley Robinson foiled an attempt by Chatham's Whites to define school boundaries by reference to the absence or presence of Blacks. By 1883 the pressure brought change and some schools were desegregated. Eight years later Chatham's last segregated school was closed.

Desegregation cannot be credited solely to black pressure or white enlightenment. The decreasing black population — the Canadian total dropped from 21,394 in 1881 to 17,437 in 1901 — was an important factor. After the Civil War as many as sixty per cent of Ontario's Blacks returned to the United States on a reverse but open "underground railway".

Many Ontario churches were unofficially segregated. In some areas there were churches with separate, back pews called, on occasion, "Nigger Heaven". Black church services were thought by many Whites to lack intellectual content, and were believed to be too emotional in appeal. Apparently, God's approval was not the point.

Actually, many Blacks preferred their own church service — usually Baptist. There they found identity, friendship, cohesion, and leadership. Historically, black Canadian churchmen often provided black brethren with their only, if often ineffective, leadership. Patience, resignation and a better day in heaven were emphasized.

In 1891, when Shadd was twenty-one, a black organization called the Kent County Civil Rights League was formed to fight racism in the area. In nearby Raleigh a black mob fought police with knives and ready guns. The "law" had been called in to rescue a young white girl who, reportedly, had been forced to carry a black man's child. During the scuffle one policeman was killed and seven Blacks arrested. One policeman threatened to burn down all the neighbouring Blacks' homes if the culprit were not apprehended. Dozens of white "vigilantes" drove their buggies to the black man's home where he was captured. (Ironically, his name was Freeman.) Later, several hundred white citizens surrounded the town's courthouse shouting, "Hang the nigger!"

In spite of prejudice and segregation the Shadds and many other black families raised their children in relative seclusion and tranquility. The Shadd family apparently escaped the heavy poverty that characterized most nineteenth century black Canadian families. According to the school treasurer's records, Grandfather Abraham had often lent money to keep open "the Shadd School".

Why did the young Shadd leave Chatham? There he had the company of family — a proud family of significant accomplishments — and, if he wished, association with many of his own colour. It was also in Chatham that Canada's most famous abolitionist meeting took place. On October 17, 1859, John Brown (who later attacked Harper's Ferry, Virginia) met with thirty-four Blacks and twelve Whites to plan strategies against Southern slaveholders. However, as the numbers of the fugitives increased and Blacks got "thick as crows" there was a pronounced antipathy toward them. In nearby Dresden, for example, the black population rose so significantly that the settlement was often called "Nigger Hole". As we shall see, Shadd's was a questing spirit and it is likely that his departure for a prairie frontier resulted less from a wish to escape the area's racism than from a search for adventure.

Whatever his motives for leaving Chatham his 1896 arrival in Kinistino created a small sensation as curious white children greeted the black teacher. According to one account a little girl sat on the teacher's knee and lifted her moistened finger to his cheek. He smilingly assured her that the colour could not be removed. His ready laughter and disciplined energy were to be valued by his pupils. Of the 433 teachers employed in the Territories' 366 schools which served 12,796 students in 1896, Shadd most probably was the only Black.

The Territorial Government recognized that the public school system was one of the most powerful agencies for the encouragement of immigration. The schoolhouse was one of the first structures to be built in the West's newly settled communities.

In addition to his value as a teacher, Shadd's limited medical knowledge became a decided advantage. Although the Kinistino Whites had originally questioned how much a black teacher could know about medicine, their doubts vanished after a Birch Hills man, whose head had been split open in an accident, was brought to Shadd's school. Students were quickly dismissed and the educator tended to the injured man who lived to thank the young "doctor".

Perhaps such experiences persuaded Shadd to return to Toronto to complete his medical studies. Earlier, when he had begun his studies at the University of Toronto, a few white students had stoutly refused to sit beside him. Shadd gave them two choices: to accept him or fight him. His powerful frame was enough to command acceptance.

After his 1898 graduation he returned to the Northwest Territories where his friends, the Lowries, helped him to build his office, a two-room log structure. He named his bedroom the

"Chamber of Silence", and his office the "Chamber of Horrors". His former landlady, Mrs. Lowrie, often acted in the role of anesthetist.

Not far from Shadd's town there lived a Cree Indian named Ne-Gue-Nan-Sew and his wife Tannis (Daughter of the South Wind) whose infant children had died of a mysterious illness. The couple's baby girl was examined by Shadd who performed an operation on what he called "the tubercular gland". The little girl lived, only to die with her parents in a fierce grass fire near Ethelton. Initially, of course, the Indians were puzzled by Shadd; many had never seen a Black. Among the Indians of the area he became the most respected non-Indian. Shadd served the Kinistino settlement until 1904 when he moved thirty miles east to Melfort, considered by some citizens to be the "capital" of the Carrot River Valley.

Melfort citizens had just cause for pride and optimism. In 1904 the *Melfort Moon's* publisher wrote that the valley was "becoming one of the potent factors which will assist in shaping the destiny of the west". The article contrasted the growing economy with that of four years earlier when there were only six small general stores reported in the valley. The newspaper man grandly claimed that the Carrot River was commercially navigable for more than one hundred miles of its length — a strange statement to this writer who spent youthful hours in the river's cool and beautiful, but limited waters.

Earlier in 1904 the *Moon* had reported that only limited homestead land was left in the valley. The editorial claimed that "all the district is prosperous, contented, and hopeful" and "business men are keen, energetic and progressive". The Canadian Northern Railway "had penetrated this great valley" making Melfort an important centre on the Winnipeg to Edmonton rail line. In a call for more people the editor wrote: "In short, this grand district requires nothing but the willing, active, enlightened, determined labour and enterprise of those who may come later." The optimism of the Saskatchewan settlers was not unique. In the same year Prime Minister Sir Wilfrid Laurier said that "it is Canada that shall fill the twentieth century".

People like Shadd were attracted by such optimism. Settlers of many nationalities were to pour into the valley. In 1905 the

Moon reported that a party of Mennonites, "the people who build the big white house and red barns," purchased 40,000 acres north of Melfort. In that year many farmers averaged forty-eight bushels of wheat per acre in what was called by a local real estate officer, "The Garden of the West". A 1907 *Moon* editorial proudly proclaimed Melfort to be "the centre of the greatest hard wheat area, taking in forty miles north, sixty miles east, fifty miles west to fifty miles south, there are 10,000 square miles or 6,400,000 acres of land". Tomorrows were beautiful and challenging.

The railroad had become the economic life-line to the rest of Canada and the world. As one account stated: "From early morning until dark the wagons with their tall boxes draw into the elevator yards, and deposit their yellow cargoes." Although the train had become a part of the landscape and a part of the romance of Canadian life, not everyone in the turn-of-the-century West was in love with it. A 1909 prairie fire at Elstow, Saskatchewan ignited by sparks from the Grand Freight Pacific Railroad caused many farmers to curse the train. Rail passengers could be equally condemnatory. A black porter (at the time there were no black conductors on Canadian railroads) serving the eighteen American landbuyers on board, described the ride on the Erwood-Melfort line: "She would roll and roll; and then when you thought she had stopped rollin' she would roll some mo'."

For some time Shadd practised medicine in his Melfort pharmacy. An advertisement for the store seems comical today:

> Central Drug Store
> Try BOZES liniment
> The Best in Saskatchewan
> For Man or Beast
> Afterwards Smoke a
> "Bonaparte" Cigar
>
> *Melfort Moon*, July 6, 1904

In matters of medicine Shadd collaborated with Dr. Thomas Charles Spence (1854-1923), one of the first doctors (some reports incorrectly claim Shadd to be the first) to serve the Carrot River Valley.

Shadd's love of life included the need to learn. In August,

1904 the *Moon* announced that he had departed for Europe where he would spend some time at "medical college in Edinburgh and Paris". The following April the paper reported that he had returned and "fitted up a suite of offices over Code's Flour and Feed Store . . . where he can be found by those requiring his services". After his return he sold his drugstore on Burrows Avenue.

The doctor's wizardry was often reported in the *Moon*, a 1905 issue recording that, initially, he had "tapped a patient's chest for 130 ounces of liquid" this amounting eventually to "nearly 300 ounces in total". Fifty-five years after the doctor's death, W. A. Aikenhead, a long-time Melfort resident, wrote of him:

> I will never forget Dr. Shadd sitting beside my little sister keeping her swathed in cool cloths and wrapped in cotton batting and oiled silk when the measles went back in on her. She had to learn to walk all over again but he saved her. Rain or snow, road or no road didn't stop the doctor. If there was no trail for the buggy or cutter he would take to horseback.

Like other doctors of that time Shadd often took his services to his patients.

The 1906 to 1911 Minute Book from Lady Minto Hospital in Melfort reveals that as one of Saskatchewan's first coroners Shadd "examined a young Scotsman who died at Fisher's restaurant" and "examined a man with a mysterious broken neck, found hidden in the straw near Bagley". Shadd's professional life received more press attention that that of other doctors, probably because of his friendship with the local editor.

Friendship did not stop Shadd from forcefully expressing his views. When Lady Minto was no more than a proposal he argued with those laymen who he felt placed the patients' welfare anywhere but first. An examination of the Minute Book reveals his influence on the institution. At the 1906 founding meeting of the board he recommended that the hospital be incorporated as a government institution. His suggestion that public donations be solicited for building purposes gained the generous support of the Carrot River pioneers. Calico balls, tag days, skating carnivals, drama nights, and other events were held to raise money. Donations arrived from all parts of the valley.

As a practical man he became directly involved in the building plans for the hospital. The Minute Book records that at early board meetings the doctor made motions regarding concrete foundations, suggested that "tender be issued for fifteen cords of wood of sound dry white poplar or spruce, four feet long," moved that "we lay in a supply of ice," and that "another coat of plaster be put on the hospital". The building's architect received the handsome sum of fifty dollars — again a result of Shadd's motion to the board.

By 1909 his medical report to the board stated that there was "an excellent institution in our midst". In that year he recommended that a ward carriage for dressing and "regularly used instruments" be purchased by the board and that ambulance costs be paid by the patients.

He quarrelled with the hospital administration who wanted to build a nurses' residence, because, he felt that money should be spent first on improvements to the hospital. He lost the argument: the residence was completed in 1910. Shadd believed that the directors had "meddled" with doctors' charges and claimed that the daily rates of $1.50, $2.00, and $2.50 were too high for his patients. Other doctors agreed. The minutes of a 1910 hospital board meeting add further insight:

> Shadd then spoke at some length first stating there had been some friction in the past between the Board and himself, but this he thought had been much exaggerated by gossiping report. He, however, looked at the hospital from a medical standpoint while the Directors, in his opinion, looked after the financial side too closely.
>
> *Minute Book,* January 20, 1910

In Shadd's day, as now, doctors did not always get along with superintendents of nurses. Lady Minto's first superintendent, Miss Heales, described in one report as a careful manager and "estimable young lady," had left "with her gift of a gold watch". Her successor and Shadd quarrelled often. He personally rebuked her for allowing smoking on the wards and complained that his prescriptions "were not promptly dealt with" by the senior nurse. He added that he wouldn't place a serious case in the hospital if the new superintendent were in charge. The "genial" doctor had his bad days! Perhaps his rheumatism was bothering him that day. That affliction, aggravated by the area's winter climate, sometimes forced the young doctor to bed. However, he liked his reputation of never being "sick a day".

A day in the country helped to calm Shadd's nerves. His 1906 red Reo, perhaps the first automobile in the area, was a familiar sight in the beautiful park belt. He gained a reputation as a fast driver. "The Reo car," he once said whimsically, "saved more people than it killed." In an area that had fewer roads than fences the latter were often "crashed through" by the black man in the red Reo en route to a serious case. A 1912 Melfort news item reported the errors of such drivers: "Complaints have been made of persons exceeding the speed limit of ten miles per hour" adding that some "travelled at a 30-mile-an-hour clip". Roads and streets were difficult by today's standards. A 1904 *Moon* item revealed that "our streets are muddy — about two inches of sky juice fell Monday".

In spite of bad weather, difficult roads, and his busy schedule, Shadd travelled to meet the needs of his patients. Residents of Fort à la Corne (on the Saskatchewan River), Lost River (region), Eldersley, Birch Hills, Yellow Creek, Star City, Ridgedale (district), and Gronlid became familiar with Shadd's skill, exuberance, and dedication.

In 1901 Shadd had run unsuccessfully for the Northwest Territories Assembly. By 1905 he favoured Saskatchewan's entry into Confederation but demanded decentralized government and strong provincial control over policies directly involving the province. He bitterly opposed Walter Scott as premier, believing that the scholarly Ford Macleod lawyer and Provincial Rights leader, Frederick Haultain, should have been asked to form the province's first government. It can be argued that Haultain was the West's greatest and most respected political leader in the twenty years following the 1885 Riel Rebellion.

Like many black Canadian families, the Shadds had long supported the Conservative Party. As a Provincial Rights candidate in the 1905 election Shadd was opposed by Liberal Thomas Sanderson, a former scout in the 1885 Riel Rebellion, and friend who later helped the doctor begin his cattle breeding operation. In his election speeches the doctor-politician stressed (1) stronger provincial government, (2) Hudson Bay railway construction, (3) taxes for the Canadian Pacific Railway, (4) provincial control of public lands, forests, and minerals, (5) local control of schools, but with a curriculum that would make "good Canadian citizens of incoming races and creeds". The Conservative leader and Shadd were angered by what they considered to be federal indifference to the West.

Shadd was an eloquent public speaker who showed courtesy to his political opponents. His heavy moustache could not hide his wide smile which flashed easily and often. In November, 1905, the *Moon* described him as "a fluent and forceful speaker" who could "rouse his audiences to the wildest pitch of enthusiasm when on a political campaign". His sense of humour and grasp of fundamental issues appealed to many voters.

The winter of 1905-06 was a very cold one with forty below zero (°F) weather common. Because of difficulties caused by the severe weather, all ballots were not counted for several weeks. On December 20, 1905, the *Moon* reported that Shadd was leading in the election. On January 3, 1906, it predicted that the Liberal would win, but acknowledged that "the doctor had put up a plucky fight." It was rumoured that "some of Scott's Liberals" had dumped two ballot boxes into the frozen North Saskatchewan River. In any case, Saskatchewanites (male only) came close to electing a black man to their first elected legislature; Sanderson defeated Shadd by fifty-two votes.

Not until 1963 did Canadians elect a Black to a provincial legislature. The Etobicoke Liberal lawyer, Leonard Braithwaite, gained that distinction in Ontario. The following year, another Black, Lincoln Alexander was elected Progressive Conservative Member of Parliament for the Ontario riding of Hamilton West.

The defeated politician remained a staunch conservative and Haultain supporter for the rest of his life. In 1906, for example, he addressed an election meeting in his birthplace, West Kent, Ontario, where he "made a very favourable impression".

Shadd's views and hopes were expressed in *The Carrot River Journal;* he was owner-editor from 1908 to 1912. During that time he was considered one of the finest editorial writers in the West. He was as eloquent in print as he was with his "large and penetrating speaking voice". His editorials spoke of Western rights, freight rates, grain prices — all topics still very much alive today. As might be expected, the irrepressible Shadd's editorials supported the Conservative Party. (Unfortunately, during his term as editor there was considerably less news printed about Shadd himself.)

He enjoyed his membership in All Saints Anglican church which he served as warden. Among others, he paid for the bells of the church built in 1906. It was in that church that he married the attractive Miss Simpson, a local white girl. The marriage produced two children, the light-skinned Garrison and the dark-skinned Louena.

The Shadd's guests met with a warm welcome. Visiting dignitaries such as Frederick Haultain looked forward to good food and good conversation at the Shadd residence. In 1911, for instance, the *Moon* reported that: "The Ven. Archdeacon Dewdeney . . . will be the guest of Dr. and Mrs. Shadd while in town." Mrs. Shadd's name appeared frequently in the newspaper's social column. The family was even able to afford to advertise for "a good smart girl" to serve as maid.

It appears that the family was considered part of the "upper crust" of the young Saskatchewan town of four hundred people. It is equally apparent that Shadd's healthy financial position and his medical practice helped to place him in the social register.

It was fortunate that Mrs. Shadd, a former bookkeeper, "kept the books" for Shadd spent and invested often. Frequently, he refused payment from those in financial difficulty, although his eye for a dollar seldom failed him. His medical practice, his drugstore, his newspaper career, and his farming activities left him with few financial worries.

On his first farm near Kinistino, which he had purchased in 1902, he experimented with growing crab apples — a significant achievement for that time and place. Later, he purchased land north and east of Melfort where his interest in agriculture came to full flower. A news item titled "Doctor Finds Profit in Mixed Farming" indicates Shadd's love of his farm:

Dr. A. S. Shadd is one of the greatest mixed farming enthusiasts in the district. He has not been in the business a great while, but he has surely grabbed the

55

big idea right off the bat. On his farm 18 miles northwest of town the doctor has 150 hogs of varying ages. He also has 98 head of finest beef cattle, rolling fat, which will bring a snug sum in the spring . . . raises all his own feed, employs competent help, and believes there is nothing so desirable and profitable in this district as mixed farming.

Melfort Moon, November 5, 1913

His proud possession was a great white bull, Bandsman's Choice, which was a prize winner at the Toronto Exhibition. The purchase price of $1,000 might indicate that Shadd was in a sound financial position. In any case, he loved cattle breeding almost as much as he loved medicine. Often he served as a veterinarian, on one occasion delivering two "babies" to the same family — a baby boy in the farmhouse, a baby calf in the barn.

The gentleman farmer became a founder and first president of the Melfort Agricultural Society. Early records of the organization indicate that Shadd's leadership was respected and solicited. He also helped to form the Farmers' Elevator Company.

As a town councilman he travelled to other Saskatchewan centres to learn how best to install sewer and water works and consistently urged council and citizens alike to "move into the twentieth century". When the town gained electricity to light its homes and streets Shadd was delighted. A 1913 Melfort news item boasted that the lights "loomed up gloriously . . . from any point of the compass". Shadd quipped: "I now feel like paying my taxes with a light heart." In the same year the citizens of Melfort and district gathered to celebrate the opening of the new post office. Because of his involvement and leadership, Shadd was honoured with the first post office box.

In 1914, led by Shadd, the town began a tree growing and town beautification programme. Some of those trees stand today as silent statements of other people's efforts. Shadd was also an active member of the Masonic Order, the Independent Order of Forresters, and the Loyal Orange Lodge. Indeed, the July 12 Orangemen's parade with its marching bands and Union Jacks was a highlight of his year. The "black Orangeman", as he jokingly called himself on occasion, was a loyal supporter of king and country.

But would he have re-examined his belief in the British Empire if he had known about William Hall, the third Canadian and first Black to win the Victoria Cross. In 1901, that Crimean War hero, described as "a brave pickaninny", was buried in an unmarked Nova Scotia grave. What would Shadd's sentiments have been if he had known that his black Canadian brothers were to fight and die in segregated army units in France? In 1914 when eighteen local men left by train to fight the Kaiser Shadd was at the station to see them off. As the train left Melfort no one on that autumn morning was more proud to be a Canadian.

Western Canada's first black doctor died early and quickly. In March, 1915, Dr. T. C. Spence and Mrs. Shadd took the failing man to a Winnipeg hospital. He had been stricken with acute appendicitis, then a serious affliction; he died shortly after an operation. One can only surmise that his energy and health were, in part, drained by nearly twenty years of relentless activity and pursuit of his goals. In his forty-five years he had tasted life fully. He had come a long way from his one-room, racially segregated, log school house in Ontario. In his short life the educator, doctor, farmer, politician, druggist, editor, civic leader, and citizen had touched and moved those with whom he made contact. A warm newspaper tribute, titled "A Friend in Need", makes the point:

> There were many little anecdotes told at the Board of Trade meeting the other night in testimony of the many acts of kindness and unflinching courage of the late Dr. Shadd, in fulfilling his duties as physician to the vast district of the Carrot River Valley, especially before the advent of the railway and telephone. How he would attend with faithfulness the poorest of his patients and would not receive a cent in return for his labours and in many cases only charging a nominal fee to others. He was the ideal country doctor, making himself a friend of the families he attended and was highly respected by all who knew him however much they may have differed from his views. . . . He was universally liked by all who knew him, especially those who received medical treatment from him, it being as good as medicine to hear his

hearty laughter when he was cheering up a patient. No matter how cold the night, he always answered the summons for his assistance, and many a night with the thermometer around zero and below, he has come in from a long drive to find another call awaiting him and he has gone without his rest and visited the patient when he, himself, had been suffering extreme pain that would make other men take to their beds.

Melfort Moon, March 15, 1915

A witness described Shadd's funeral as "easily the largest gathering of this nature that has been held in the Carrot River Valley." And, one elderly resident, W. A. Aikenhead, reminisces in a letter to the author:

I well remember the funeral of Dr. Shadd. There wasn't room in the church. There were more outside the church than in the church. The casket was in the cemetery when the last of the procession had not left the town. This is a distance of two miles and that is still the largest funeral ever held in Melfort.

The Masonic funeral procession, accompanied by the town band playing the "Death March" made its way on muddy roads to Mount Pleasant Cemetery. There, a large group of Shadd's friends, Indians, ("out of place" at the church), waited to pay respects to the departed spirit.

It was said in 1972 by a ninety-year-old pioneer that Shadd once told him of his three ambitions: to become a doctor, to become a member of parliament, and to marry a white woman. Shadd's ambitions were obviously wider than the old pioneer's dubious account indicates.

To today's black militants Shadd might seem to have been "another Uncle Tom" — black on the outside, white on the inside. He should be viewed as a remarkable Canadian without reference to colour. After Alfred's death his brother wrote of the doctor's brand of Canadianism:

Shadd's family name has been without exception associated with conservatism and we feel that especially in this hour of the Empire's need we have lost a valiant leader and an able and worthy exponent of the best British principles.

Melfort Moon, March 19, 1915

If Shadd was, indeed, "white on the inside" he was no "Uncle Tom". He was too self-assured, too dynamic, and above all, too proud to be subservient to anyone. He was more than a fine example of the country doctor now missed by many Canadians.

After publicly thanking the community for its kindness Shadd's widow took the children to live in Ontario. Meanwhile, citizens of the valley went on making a living and fighting a war. It is doubtful that they could immediately measure Shadd's full impact.

It is equally doubtful that his white friends knew of the private hurts he suffered. Greatly interested in public affairs he almost certainly would have read newspaper accounts of the lynchings and brutalities endured by others of his colour in the United States. He would have read, too, of the often unfriendly reception given to the nearly one thousand Blacks who came to the Canadian prairies between 1908 and 1911. That migration, originally feared to be only part of a much larger group, posed a threat to the solid white citizens. Shadd, however, was no threat; one Black could not threaten blood "purity", a concept very important to early Westerners. Furthermore, he had the talents and characteristics needed by pioneer settlers who often paid him the naive compliment: "Doc, you're as good as any white man."

Some will consider the symbolism of Melfort's Mount Pleasant Cemetery where Shadd has rested for half a century. At one end of his grave stands a white-barked birch, at the other end a black-barked poplar. Beneath the tall branches, which still do not touch, sits a headstone of black Canadian granite.

That Shadd was respected as a person has been established. But his story is of one Black in an otherwise white (excluding Indians) community. His colour presented little problem because he was one person. Had there been a thousand Shadds in the district would the situation have been different?

CRIMINALS AND CHARACTERS

Crimes, like virtues, are their own rewards.

—George Farquhar

It would be misleading to suggest that *all* Blacks on the Western Canadian frontier were model citizens. They were people — just that — not inherently inferior or superior, but equal, and subject to the same frailties as any people. Black pioneers numbered amongst themselves proportionately no fewer criminals (and no more) than any immigrant group. But, like scattered chunks of hard coal on the prairie snow, they were highly visible. The unfortunate consequence of this visibility was the tendency of Western Whites to project onto all Blacks the criminal characteristics of the few.

Nigger Dan Williams

The Arrival

One of the wildest and most feared men of the early Canadian West was "Nigger Dan" Williams, a simple-minded, giant Black who recognized only two authorities: God, and Queen Victoria. When he began work with the Hudson's Bay Company, he believed he had a contract with the Queen. The known facts of his life often outstrip the legend. The latter, however, was used by settlers to chase children to bed or to threaten them: "You better be good or Nigger Dan will get you!"

Legend suggests that Dan Williams, along with "Nigger Joe" Potter, came from the Deep South where "Lincoln's soldiers" first freed them from slavery, and then tore apart the lifestyle they had known and hated. The story suggests that the ex-slave left his wife in the Deep South "to move to freedom" in Canada's North-West. He arrived in the Peace River country in 1869.

It seems more probable that Dan was born in Kingston in Canada West. There are suggestions that he served as a handyman-cook with the famous Captain John Palliser expedition which was to examine the feasibility of railway construction from Lake Superior to the Rockies, and to report on the agricultural potential of the southern districts of Rupert's Land. Many Whites believed that Black men learned Indian languages and dialects very quickly, and were particularly attractive to Indian women. Perhaps Palliser had a "public relations" purpose if, in fact, he did actually employ the black man.

Dan loved the North-West. Perhaps his rather simple mind was attracted by name, "Peace River". One wonders if he might have been afraid of "Slave Lake". In any case, the name Dan Williams became known from Fort St. John to Fort Dunvegan to Fort Vermillion to Fort Edmonton. His name was undoubtedly a conversation topic around many tables during the 1870s and 1880s. His exploits became more fabulous with each telling; a legend grew.

The Legend

Throughout the land of the Beaver Indians, Williams, who

was barely literate, carried his Bible on all occasions. Sometimes he baptised Indians — both parties obviously unsure of the ceremony. His Bible, it has been said, once stopped a bullet fired at him by angry miners in the Peace River country. Without benefit of clergy, Williams took as his wife, Thela, daughter of the Beaver chief, Komaxala.

The Beavers and their chief were mystified by Williams' skin colour. He was considered a "black spirit" who might have "special medicine", both good and evil. Williams was aware that his "medicine" came from his Sharps rifle, a weapon with which he had fantastic skill. On one occasion, his rifle saved Komaxala's life after the chief had been attacked by a huge bear. The Beavers could then at least partially overlook Williams' ineptitude as a fisherman and trapper.

During a hunting expedition Williams' bride-to-be was struck by lightning and left mute. The incident demonstrated to the Beavers that the black man's presence angered the gods, and they were displeased with Williams' behaviour during the hunt; he insisted on killing wolves which were driving cariboo in the direction of the hunters. Furthermore, the Indians respected animal life and could not appreciate Dan's loud laughter after an animal had fallen to his bullets. They did acknowledge his courage when he saved Thela from certain drowning. She then belonged to him; she was mute and of little value to the tribe. Dan and Thela left the Beaver Indians and spent years exploring the rivers, creeks, forests and lakes of the Peace River area.

The quarrelsome Williams found himself perennially at odds with miners, trappers, the Royal North West Mounted Police and the Hudson's Bay Company. When he argued, his rifle often spoke the last word. Stories suggest that Williams' gun eventually brought him to the rope in Fort Saskatchewan. After an argument with a Hudson's Bay Company factor over fur prices, Dan told his friend, "Banjo Mike" McGinnis, that a well-placed rifle shot would properly frighten the company official. With casual but frighteningly skilled aim, Dan fired his Sharps. The bullet, as he had said it would, struck the door joint six inches from the factor's head. Another cause for raucous laughter!

The incident quickly brought the N.W.M.P. who took Dan to his trial in Fort Saskatchewan. There, he was met by his old friend "Banjo Mike" McGinnis. The Irishman claimed that Dan had not attempted to kill the H.B.C. official. He is credited with this defense of his friend, Dan:

> Anyone who knows anything about bullets will tell you that from the sound made by a passing bullet it is impossible to tell whether it is a foot or a yard or ten or twenty yards away. And surely if the defendant had intended doing bodily harm, and the bullet from his rifle did pass close to the plaintiff's ear, the house at least would have been hit, as he, the plaintiff, admits that he was standing at the door in front of the house; yet, mark you, he does not admit knowing whether the house was hit; why so, gentlemen, I leave you to decide. But let me tell you this, that I know, as many other miners know, that Dan Williams, at a distance of one hundred yards, can take the eye out of a jack-rabbit at every pop. Gentlemen, had Dan Williams had the slightest intention of harming McKinlay, he would not have been here today to tell you the amusing little story whereby he gives you credit for some sense of humour without paying you much of a compliment for intelligence.

Quite an impressive speech from a man of limited training.

Other parts of the legend tell of Williams' arrest for murder and attempted murder. Police entered his cabin, and, in their haste, shot Thela in the heart. It was claimed that the mute woman had jumped in front of Dan to save his life. Just before being shot, she shouted, "Tea-kwa" ("Stop") — her first and last words subsequent to being struck by lightning. Dan's reaction was predictable: he shot the police officer dead.

The lugubrious Williams surrendered to other officers. Not until he was later denied a visit to Thela's grave did he fight his captors. It took six men to hold and shackle him. He was then taken on the long winter's journey to Fort Saskatchewan for this March, 1880 trial at which he was found guilty of murder. The legend continued: Daniel Williams, killer, marched to the gallows, Bible in hand. His neck broke immediately after the springing of the trap. His soul departed for Hell.

The Facts Interpreted

Most of what is known about "Nigger Dan" Williams is like a tangled length of barbed wire: the barbs are sharp; the wire cannot be completely untangled.

The huge, dull, but cunning, black man might be described as "barbarous". His peculiar guile forced him to defend violently what he considered his own. His physical and emotional energies dwarfed his intelligence.

Throughout his life he quarrelled with the law. The best-known documented incident involved one William Butler (later Sir William), a Tipperary Irish soldier who, in the 1869-70 Riel uprising, had served as an intelligence officer. Butler knew the Canadian West's loneliness and remoteness in the 1870s better than most people. His incredible dog-team and horseback journeys from Winnipeg to the mountains in the winters of 1871 and 1873 gave rise to some of Canada's best travel literature: *The Great Lone Land* and *The Wild North Land*. His greatest embarrassment was Dan Williams.

On the south shore of the Peace River there stood a tumbledown fort, St. John, a remote settlement in an area which was itself remote. To the west were the towering white peaks of the Rocky Mountains; to the east, south, and north a seemingly endless mixed wilderness of pine, stream, lake, and prairie. Such forts were welcome sights to the weary prairie traveller who might have gone for weeks without seeing another human being.

On arriving at the fort, however, Butler's pleasure was tempered by the presence of Nigger Dan Williams. Williams claimed that the Hudson's Bay Company fort of St. John was built on land he had earlier claimed as his own.

The confrontation between the cultivated soldier of British Empire tradition, and the suspected murderer, thief, and troublemaker, took place in April of 1873 in the depths of the Canadian wilderness. According to Butler's account, Williams "from his lair . . . issued manifestoes of a very violent nature . . . and planted stakes . . . upon which he painted in red ochre hieroglyphics of a menacing character". At night, the giant Black stood on the river's shore cursing his enemies and reciting approximations of verses from his Bible.

Storage of slaves aboard the *Brooks* of Liverpool, illustration from Clarkson's *Abstract of the Evidence*, 1791.

The Canadian artist François Malepart de Beaucourt painted this portrait of his black servant, now known as *Portrait of a Negro Slave*, in 1786. McCord Museum, Montreal.

Congo slave coffle en route to sale by Arabs, ca. 1870. The Science Museum, London.

South Carolina slave quarters, ca. 1860 (similar to first home of John Ware). Lightfoot Collection.

Alberta rangemen. Glenbow-Alberta Institute, Calgary.

Daniel Lewis family, perhaps the first black family of Alberta, ca. 1900. Left to right standing: Alberta, Ellie (Ethel), Jessie, Frances, Mary Octavia, Daniel; left to right seated: Daniel, Charlotte, Spencer. Photo courtesy Janet Ware.

Mildred, Robert, Janet (Nettie) and John Ware, 1896. Glenbow-Alberta Institute, Calgary.

John Ware's sons Arthur and William in Canadian Army uniforms,
World War I. Glenbow-Alberta Institute, Calgary.

The Ware home near Brooks, Alberta, ca. 1896. John Ware is on horseback, Mildred and baby Nettie on porch. Photo courtesy Janet Ware.

John Ware and friend. Glenbow-Alberta Institute, Calgary.

Alfred Schmitz Shadd, M.D., C.M. (1870-1915). Private collection.

Alfred Schmitz Shadd. Private collection.

"Auntie" with Colonel James Macleod's children. Glenbow-Alberta
Institute, Calgary.

Frontiersman and police scout Jerry Potts who led the capture of the Bond Gang. Glenbow-Alberta Institute, Calgary.

Negro-Blackfoot interpreter David Mills on Blood Reserve (near Lethbridge) with Chief One Spot, Head Chief Red Crow, agent Pocklington (seated) and missionary Cowan, ca. 1896. Glenbow-Alberta Institute, Calgary.

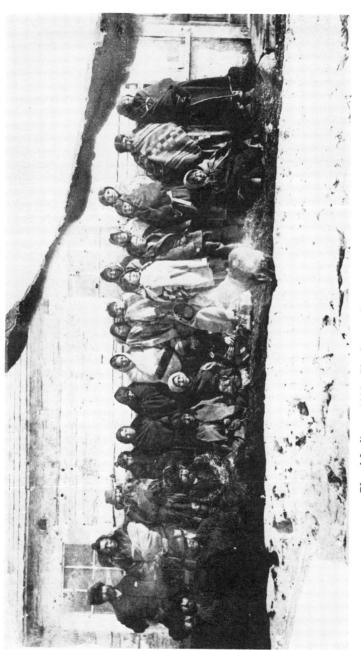

Blood Indians, 1880. Glenbow-Alberta Institute, Calgary.

Jefferson Davis Edwards, Amber Valley farmer. Glenbow-Alberta Institute, Calgary.

He had decided that a young Hudson's Bay Company factor, George Kennedy, was responsible for all his trouble. On April 12, 1873, Williams issued the following ultimatum:

> Kenedy I hear by
> Worne you that Com and Gett your
> persnol property if eny you
> have Got of my prmeeis In 24 hours and then keep away
> from me because I shal Not betrubbled Nor trod on
> only be her most Noble
>   Majesty
>   Government
>   (Sgd) D. T. WILLIAMS

On the back of the note Williams added: "I have wated longe A-day for an ancer from that Notis you toer-Down and now It is my turn to tore down."

That both Williams and Kennedy appealed to Butler as Justice of the Peace embarrased the "lawman" (as the Black described him). Butler gave grudging respect to the "Black Bismark" whose rifle was capable of upsetting any judicial decision. Butler's response was a masterpiece in vagueness:

JUDICIAL MEMORANDUM

> Various circumstances having occurred in the neighbourhood of the Hudson's Bay Fort known as St. John's, on the Peace River, of a nature to lead to the assumption that a breach of the peace is liable to arise out of the question of disputed ownership in a plot of land on the north side of the river, on which the Hudson's Bay Company has erected buildings to serve as their future place of business, and on which it is asserted one Daniel Williams, a person of colour, formerly lived, this is to notify all persons concerned in this question, that no belief of ownership, no former or present possession, will be held in any way to excuse or palliate the slightest infringement of the law, or to sanction any act of violence being committed, or to occasion any threats being made use

65

of by any of the said parties which might lead to a breach of the peace.

Executed by me, as Justice of Peace for Rupert's Land and the North-West, this 22nd day of April, 1873.

SIGNED, etc. etc.

Butler believed that Williams was impressed by the tenor of the memorandum, and that the word "executed" carried with it "a sense of profound strangulation" to the black man.

The Fort St. John incident was discussed by settlers for many years to come. Few believed that the memorandum would stop the mercurial Williams. But in the end, perhaps, Butler won. It was his report that supported John A. Macdonald's plan to establish the North-West Mounted Police, who later chased and arrested the "black demon".

The *Saskatchewan Herald* received reports of the "Nigger Dan" incident as late as 1879. Little is known of Dan's activities immediately after the Butler memorandum. An Edmonton newspaper correspondent displayed hesitant admiration, if not sympathy, for Dan in his frequent difficulties with the N.W.M.P. and the Hudson's Bay Company. The newspaper reported that Williams " has been making things hot for the Hudson's Bay Company on Peace River again". Dan had set fire to Hudson's Hope, a small post near the mountains. Before the arrival of the N.W.M.P. Dan "skipped out and had his gun with him".

But the police caught their man and took him to Fort Saskatchewan for trial. On his way to custody he was left overnight in an H.B.C. storehouse at Shaftesbury Flats. Always anxious to voice his innocence, he carved into the storehouse door: "Daniel Williams, prisner of Her Majesty under fals pretenses." Poor Williams. He must have thought that even the Queen had deserted him in times of trouble.

Initially, Williams received a degree of public support. A reporter noted that he had been "pretty roughly handled by the company". As more information became known about him the tone of the reports changed. He was described as "a real tartar" with "a ten year's outfit of criminal charges against him". In August, 1879, the *Saskatchewan Herald* reported:

NIGGER DAN

This notorious individual . . . was arrested at Peace River for shooting and maiming three horses, the property of the Hudson's Bay Company — one of which died, a second was permanently injured, and the third recovered. A second charge is that he set fire to a storehouse containing an immense quantity of gunpowder belonging to the Hudson's Bay Company in April last. He was arrested for this offense, and when on his way in he made his escape, and the fact of his having fired upon his guards with both his rifle and revolver while doing so was made the ground of a third charge against him. A preliminary examination was had and a *prima facie* case made out; but as Dan said some witnesses on his behalf were on the way he was remanded for eight days.

Saskatchewan Herald, August 25, 1879

One of the witnesses was "Banjo Mike" McGinnis, Williams' best friend. Like Williams, the red-headed Irish trapper, gold-miner, and criminal gained a measure of public admiration for his "I don't give a damn" attitude toward life and law. He travelled widely in the West and could appear suddenly at such scattered outposts as Fort Carleton, Fort Edmonton, Fort Macleod, Fort Walsh, and Fort St. John in the Peace River country. He deserved the early West's simple encomium: "He was a good traveller."

It is doubtful that the court took Mike's testimony very seriously. He was considered a "character," a source of amusement and trouble. In spite of his and Dan's protestations, Williams was sent to jail. It appears that he was treated lightly by the law:

In the case of the Crown against Dan Williams for shooting horses belonging to the Hudson's Bay Company at St. John, Peace River, the jury returned a verdict of not guilty: and in the case against Williams for shooting at James McKinlay at Fort St. John, Peace River, a similar verdict was returned. In the other charge against Williams — that of setting fire to the Hudson's Bay Company's buildings at Fort St. John — His Honour held that having been tried on two charges by a jury, and a verdict of not guilty given in both cases, it would be useless to proceed any further against him; he would therefore bind him over to appear, should the Government see fit to proceed further against him.

Saskatchewan Herald, July 5, 1880

One must wonder what the police could have thought when Williams sued them for "illegal arrest and ill-treatment". He demanded $12,000 in damages. The magistrate said that the black plaintiff had no case, and had deserved rough treatment because he had resisted arrest. With strange Solomonic logic the court decided that both sides were innocent of any wrong-doing.

Little is known about the rest of William's life. He certainly was not hanged as the legend would have one believe. It is likely that his story became confused with that of another Black, Jesse Williams, the first person hanged in Calgary.

In the spring of 1882, Dan's name appeared in the *Edmonton Bulletin* which noted rather vaguely that near Fort Saskatchewan a land-claim dispute had arisen involving property allegedly sold by Williams to one O. Dorome. In any case, Dan Williams was not a man to live in towns. He loved the wild country and returned to the land of the Beaver Indians.

Nothing else is reported of him until 1887. In July of that year, Williams' old enemy, Kennedy, told the *Edmonton Bulletin* that during the previous winter five men plus "Nigger Dan went up the Finlay branch of the Peace" where a disagreement of some sort occurred. Dan and a friend returned to the mouth of the Finlay "where they built a cabin in which to winter". Kennedy added casually that "Dad took sick . . . and gradually wasted away until he died about the middle of February".

Daniel Williams, who "recognized" only his Saviour, his Queen, and his rifle, and who believed only in himself, had found a lasting peace. While he was alive few people dared to call him by his racist nickname, "Nigger Dan". Westerners referred openly to the likes of "Sleepy Johnny" and "Windy

Ike" but those who called Dan Williams "Nigger" literally risked life and limb. His presence, real or imagined, was reason enough to be careful, even after his death. Fear could chase pioneer children to an early bed: "You better be good or Nigger Dan will get you!"

William Bond

William Bond, black whiskey trader, earned the dubious distinction of being the first person arrested by the newly-formed North-West Mounted Police, and the first person to escape their custody.

Guns, horses, technology, and disease — "benefits" of white civilization, had forever transformed the lives of the Indian society in Western Canada. More than anything, however, it was the whiskey traders who led most Indians to poverty, degradation, and self-alienation.

Vile bootleg whiskey poured into the West, especially into Alberta, along the Whoop-Up Trail, which connected Montana's "Sagebrush Sodom" (Fort Benton) to such ramshackle Canadian posts as Robbers' Roost, Whiskey Gap, Standoff, and Slideout. Fort Whoop-Up, established near today's Lethbridge, was considered the terminal point of the venture by many American whiskey traders who brought with them their rot-gut concoctions of ink, tobacco juice, peppers, molasses, tobasco, and alcohol.

In May, 1873, in the beautiful Cypress Hills, a group of American trappers and traders massacred more than thirty Indians, many of whom were drunk. The victims, led by Little Soldier, were thought to have stolen horses from a Montana trading post. The Indians' muzzle loaders were no match for the Whites' rapid-firing rifles. The resulting carnage was the deciding factor in the formation of the North-West Mounted Police. The whiskey trade became the force's assigned target.

After the twenty-four officers and 295 men made their famous and remarkably long march from Dufferin, Manitoba to their headquarters-to-be at Fort Macleod, the redcoats immediately went about their whiskey war with ready warrant and wit. Even while the fort was being built, Colonel James Macleod struck at the whiskey traders. In December, 1874 he sent the West's best tracker and scout, Jerry Potts, to capture the heavily armed Bond gang.

Three Bulls, a minor Indian Chief, had reported that with Bond he had traded horses for "fire-water" — so named because some Indians insisted that liquor should burn when touched by flame. The chief led Potts and a ten-man detachment to Pine Coulee some fifty miles north of the police headquarters. They arrested Bond along with four other traders including "Kamoose" Taylor. (Kamoose is an Indian term meaning "stealer of women".) The posse searched Bond's wagons and found whiskey, revolvers, rifles, and more than one hundred buffalo robes. The suspect whiskey was poured onto the prairie snow. Wrongly, and perhaps smugly, Macleod reported to Ottawa that the Bond adventure had signalled a "complete stoppage" of the whiskey trade. The gang was kept in jail until each member could pay a $200 fine. A crafty Fort Benton merchant, J. D. Weatherwax, paid all fines except that of the black man who remained in custody. While being transferred from one building to another, Bond escaped from Fort Macleod. A sentry fired at but missed the fleeing figure. The constable whose charge Bond had been under was reduced in rank by Macleod who immediately ordered extra fatigue parade for his men. Security was tightened. On the Sunday morning before Christmas, 1874, the chastised one-dollar-a-day police must have thought angrily about Bond, the first man to escape from them. The Mounties had gotten, but not kept, their man.

If the Fort could not contain Bond, the terrible January weather could. It appears that he froze to death in the winter snows. Perhaps his demise lessened Macleod's embarrassment.

Nigger Molly

The remarkable Colonel Macleod had further difficulty with a "Nigger Molly" who called herself the first "white" woman to settle in the Medicine Hat area. There, Molly and her partner and friend, "Tin Cup Joe," traded liquor with nearby Indians. On being apprehended Molly and Tin Cup were taken to Fort Walsh for trial where each received a stiff $250 fine.

Apparently Molly's temper was no joy to behold. In Medicine Hat the former Montana woman washed clothes for a living in competition with a white washerwoman, "Slippery Anne". Once, when very drunk, the two of them began fighting. After preliminary punches Molly grabbed her butcher knife and was about to use it on Anne when the white woman seized a pail of boiling wash water. A standoff was declared. Anne then told Molly (who was given to very rough language) to use the knife on her own tongue then to fumigate the knife. Anne's tongue was as sharp as Molly's knife.

Mills

Another Montana Black, Henry Mills, made his mark in southern Alberta. Six-apekwan (Black White Man), as he was called by the Blackfoot, was a hunter, trapper and frontiersman who guided the amazing bull trains from Fort Benton to Fort Whoop-Up. In two languages the illiterate Mills coaxed, cajoled, and cussed the plodding oxen as few others could. After marrying a Blackfoot in the early 1850s, Mills worked for the American Fur Company. He was later accepted into the Blood Indian tribe of southern Alberta where his son, David, became even better known than his father.

Long before his father's death in 1878, "Old Dave," as he came to be called, became a well-known character on the Fort Benton-Fort Whoop-Up trail. The Black-Indian bullwacker supreme was a powerfully built man who earned the respect of both Indians and Whites. Scabby Bull — his Indian name — worked for the Indian Department as an interpreter after 1880 when he settled in southern Alberta. There, he was married by Father Lacombe to his Blood bride, Poosa.

Early newspaper reports indicate the character of Mills' era. In 1887, the *Macleod Gazette* noted that "the main street was blocked with bull trains, loaded with general freight and coal". Four years later, the same source reported that the streets of Macleod were "in the normal state of filth, and ready to welcome cholera or any other pestilence which may have taken a pleasure trip west". A typical letter to the editor wanted "to draw attention to the nuisance of having one's premises constantly involved by an array of hogs that are allowed to run at large." Still other citizens complained that sleep was difficult while drunk cowboys fired their pistols into the night sky. One cowboy's revolver discharged while in its holster, killing the horse on which the cowboy was riding.

When "Old Dave" died in 1918 the *Lethbridge Herald* acknowledged the passing of the Black-Indian frontiersman:

> A real old timer passed on . . . in the person of Dave Mills. . . . Old Dave as he was known came to Alberta during the early days of the early traders. . . . His mother was a Blood woman and his father a coloured man. He acted as interpreter during the treaty at Blackfoot Crossing.

> *Lethbridge Herald*, April 11, 1918

The children and grandchildren of Mills and his second wife, Holy Rabbit Woman, still live in the area of the Belly River.

A Call For Judge Lynch

In 1884 a black ex-slave named Jesse Williams (no relation to Daniel Williams) committed one of the most blood-thirsty crimes in Calgary's history. At the time, Calgary was an up-and-coming new town with a population of 450. A visitor paid the settlement a dubious compliment:

> Calgary is the most orderly, well-regulated town I was ever in, considering the wild reckless character of many of its inhabitants. Liquor laws are most stringently enforced by the Mounted Police. . . . I saw no fights and certainly no drunken men.

> *Calgary Herald*, August 21, 1886

In 1883-84 attempts had been made to establish a telephone system in Calgary "if they can obtain twenty subscribers at $70 per year," and steps were being taken to build a school for Calgary's reported thirty children. Williams' crime was all the more "black-hearted" in the face of such attention to progress and orderliness.

The forty-three-year-old, Texas-born Williams, described by

the *Calgary Herald* as having "a little twitch in the left eye, which gives him a diabolical appearance," had worked as a cook for the Canadian Pacific Railway, the Virginia Chop House, and the Far West Hotel in Calgary. He lived with a Sarcee Indian woman known only as "Religious". Williams, Religious, and their friend, Little Chief, lived nearby among "smoke-browned teepees" which, according to the *Herald*, made a "very picturesque element in the landscape".

One of the town's merchants, a Mr. McKelvie, had hired young Scot-born James Adams to work during the evening hours. Late on a February night in 1884, Williams, reportedly "heavily liquored," visited the store where he robbed and murdered (with razor and axe) the storekeeper's assistant. A lynch mob was assembled later that night and the stable owner, in the best of Western movie tradition, offered his horses to anyone who would join the posse. The suspect was soon captured at an Indian camp about four miles from the town. The *Saskatchewan Herald* reported the "strong sentiments in favour of lynching indulged in". Some also wanted to hang the black man's companions — two "half-breeds" and two "squaws".

The trial was brief. Williams, defended by James Alexander Lougheed (grandfather of Alberta premier Peter Lougheed) remained impassive as many witnesses, including Religious, testified against him. The suspect's plea of "not guilty" was not taken seriously by the townspeople. After a five-minute deliberation, the six-man jury brought in the guilty verdict. Williams' only reaction was a complaint that he did not approve of the irons he had been forced to wear throughout the trial.

Later, in jail, the taciturn prisoner admitted his guilt. After he had partially severed his chains with a knife (no one knows its source) he was forced to wear a thirty pound ball and chain. A reporter who visited Williams described him as "nonchalant and sangfroid". Williams, a Civil War veteran, reported that his coming execution would be the third time he would face death. His statement was printed in the *Herald:*

> My crime I know to be horrible, and could any atonement of mind undo the wrong I have done, I would willingly make it. I do not grumble at my sentence but fully acknowledge its justice. I have

been spending my time in prayer and supplication
and now do not fear death, but throw myself on the
infinite mercy of God through Christ. I know that it is
hard, I think, for him to pardon me, but I hope and
trust that God will.

Calgary Herald, April 2, 1884

It is likely that the above statement credited to the barely literate
Williams had been heavily "edited" by the newspaper.

Another statement made by Williams during the same
interview casts doubt upon his sanity as, of course, does the fact
of his crime:

I was going to ask the judge to give me two
six-shooters and hold off the police, and then turn me
loose to the citizens of Calgary, as they wanted me so
badly. I would have made a short work of some of
them. After I had killed a few of them the rest would
have run and I would have made off. At any rate, if
they did kill me, it would have been better than
waiting here so long.

Calgary Herald, April 2, 1884

Williams was correct in at least one respect; many settlers
wanted "Judge Lynch" to execute him. In having held Williams
in custody, said one letter to the editor, the police force had
failed to protect the peaceful town. The anonymous citizen
added: "If they do not, they will soon find out that the citizens
both can and will ferret out these offenders and punish them in
a summary manner." It was noted that there was no shortage of
telegraph poles for such a purpose.

On March 29, 1884 the citizens of Calgary — the angry and the
curious — gathered to watch Williams' execution. A sixteen-foot
scaffold had been erected on the west side of the fort at the back
of the officers' quarters. After saying, "I am here through
drink," and vowing that he would meet his victim in heaven,
the condemned man walked with a priest to the waiting rope:

The executioner then proceeded to adjust the rope
around the criminal's neck, after which he drew on
the black cap and stood back to see that all was in
readiness. At that moment there was a breathless

silence, till, seeing everything was complete, the executioner seized an axe, and with one blow severed the rope attached to the bolt. There was a crash and the form of the wretched man disappeared below the scaffold. On going below, it was found that the fall, although about seven feet six inches, had not succeeded in breaking his neck and he struggled convulsively for the space of seven minutes. The body was allowed to remain suspended during an interval of twenty minutes, when life being quite extinct, it was cut down and placed in a coffin.

Calgary Herald, April 2, 1884

The police, the court, and the hangman had met the community's demands. The *Herald* added: "Let this be a warning to all evil-doers to amend their lives."

Bad Press

In the Williams case Calgarians sought and received quick rope justice. The crime was horrible but angers were heightened by the suspect's colour. The "bad press" received by Jesse Williams, William Bond, Daniel Williams and others did a real disservice to the thousands of peaceful Blacks who entered the meant-to-be-white West. Pioneer Justice dispensed quick punishment to the handful of black outlaws but little warm welcome to their peaceful brothers and sisters.

75

DARK SPOTS IN ALBERTA

Let us preserve for the sons of Canada the lands they propose to give to Niggers.
— House of Commons Debates, 1911

Before 1907 Oklahoma had been part of the American "Indian Territory". In that year Oklahoma's adoption of statehood precipitated an influx of white homesteaders — and the increasing segregation of Blacks. In an attempt to escape persecution a number of Blacks, slightly fewer than a thousand in all, journeyed to Western Canada, the "Promised Land" to the north. Their welcome was to be less than warm.

In the autumn of 1909 a major group of Oklahoma Blacks arrived in Saskatchewan where it became a part of the communities of Wilkie and Maidstone. Other American Blacks moved to such Alberta settlements as Amber Valley, Junkins (Wildwood), Clyde, and Breton (Keystone). Still others went to eastern Manitoba and to the Thunder Bay region. The black settlers appeared to want two things especially: land near railroads and distance from the United States.

Perhaps the West's best known black settlement was established at Amber Valley, east of Athabaska, Alberta. Led by twenty-two-year-old Jefferson Davis Edwards (named after the president of the Southern states), the several hundred Blacks formed a cohesive community. They soon built a school, church, and post-office; they put down their roots. Edwards, with his wife and ten children, became patriarch of Amber Valley.

The small, wiry gentleman says that he is "pro-Canadian all the way". He claims never to have regretted his move to Western Canada and staunchly refuses to discuss any racial problems that existed during his homesteading years. He named one son Booker after the black American educator, leader, and writer, Booker T. Washington, who represented the Accommodationist point of view. Edwards and other Blacks soon learned how "accommodating" western Canadians were to those who threatened their blood purity.

Apparently, the Blacks were encouraged to emigrate to Canada. A report from Guthrie, the former capital of Oklahoma, suggested that the "exodus of negroes" was partially sponsored by a White-owned colonization company in that state. In 1910 a Clearview, Oklahoma newspaper owned by a Black, printed an article titled "Alberta, the Home for the Colored Race". During that year numerous Blacks "scouted" the area, returning to Oklahoma and bringing their families and friends back in the following year. A 1911 report from Enid, Oklahoma, reprinted in the *Edmonton Capital*, stated in part: "Within the next few months it is estimated that at least one thousand negroes will leave from the northern and central part of this state for Alberta where they will form colonies in the vicinity of Edmonton." That they were not as welcome as they had hoped is confirmed by Winnipeg and Lethbridge newspapers of the day:

> Driven from Oklahoma, where they claim to have been robbed of property and their right to vote, a band of negroes are . . . facing the problem of being barred from western Canada, where they had hoped to start anew.
>
> *Manitoba Free Press*, March 22, 1911
> and *Lethbridge Herald*, April 11, 1911

Many Whites, such as immigration agent Jack Webster of

Edmonton, attempted to convince Blacks that the climate was too tough for "people whose native land is in tropical regions". As a Washington, D.C. dispatch informed:

> Their ability to acclimatize under temperatures that sometimes reach as low as 70 degrees below zero in the far northwest, and the responsibility of many members of the race, are complaints cited against them by the Canadians. In the Peace River Valley homesteads have been taken up by thousands of coloured people. Here the cold of winter reaches intensity, and it is not regarded as physically possible for the coloured race to thrive and prosper under conditions so foreign to its origin.
>
> Reprinted in the *Manitoba Free Press*, April 27, 1911

In 1911 immigration superintendent William Duncan Scott drew up a proposal for an Order-in-Council which would prohibit "any immigrant belonging to the Negro race, which race is deemed unsuitable for the climate and requirements of Canada" from coming to Canada for one year. The Order-in-Council was never declared but it does show the intent of some officials.

Both the Winnipeg and Edmonton Boards of Trade went on record as opposing negro immigration and suggested to Blacks that the climate and public opinion should be enough to keep them in the South. When many Blacks claimed to prefer the climate of Alberta to that of the southern United States it became necessary to find other "reasons" to keep them out.

Economic reasons were expressed by Edmonton's Trades and Labour Council in 1911. The Council passed a resolution opposing the migration as "it was amply proven that an unlimited influx of negroes into the province would invariably lower the standard of living". None of the "proof" was presented.

Indeed many of the black settlers were financially well prepared. One lady from Kansas appeared at Edmonton's 1st Street immigration hall with one thousand dollars sewn into the hem of her petticoat. Each adult black immigrant was legally obliged to have two hundred dollars on his person in order to enter the country. One group which stopped in Winnipeg en route to Edmonton was led by a man named Smeed who was "worth" $40,000 with $10,000 of it in his possession. This group of ninety-four adults (some of them former slaves) and twenty-four children, from Waleake, Oklahoma, had owned and operated farms in that state. A large number of them brought farming tools and equipment, horses and mules. Altogether, their effects and livestock filled seven railway cars. Reporting on another group a 1911 *Saskatoon Daily Phoenix* observed that "the financial standing in every case was good, averaging $300 each member, and many could show bills and drafts from $1,000 to $3,500 — no small sum in 1911. Many black farmers, then, were as solvent as their white brethren. For some Whites this solvency presented a real problem. As a Mr. Elliot of the Edmonton Lands office said of thirty Kansas Blacks who had begun to farm near Lobstick Lake: "It seems rather a pity as the land there is very good . . . but we have no means of keeping them out."

There was little reason, then, to exclude the Southern Blacks because of any danger of their becoming an economic drag on the community. Many arrived with sound economic potential. Z. W. Mitchell of the Royal Legion, Edmonton branch, admitted that Blacks "should not create any cause for uneasiness, nor should they be a menace to the morals of any community, if they make good, and are kept on their farms". Mitchell claimed that one Oklahoma group of 175 had arrived in Edmonton with capital amounting to between $75,000 and $100,000. The *Edmonton Capital* which grandly claimed that Mitchell ranked with Booker T. Washington as an authority "on the negro race problem," quoted the Legion member as saying, "I am absolutely opposed to allowing negroes to come to Canada who cannot make good."

Health reasons were the only grounds left on which Blacks could be denied entry into Canada. In Winnipeg, Blacks arriving from the South were "subjected to rigorous medical examination . . . most comprehensive in nature". A 1911 report from Emerson, Manitoba, told of Blacks being in a surly mood and angry about the nature of the personal health examination. After living in Edmonton for a year and a half, R. R. Cogburn, a black immigrant, was deported to Oklahoma — a result of his being "without means and suffering from a malady which renders him unfit to work". He was escorted to the border (south of Emerson, Manitoba) by Mr. J. Beckett, an immigration officer from Winnipeg. Cogburn's case, however, appears to be an exception. As old "Daddy" Smeed, who "spied out" the area in the summer of 1910, said: "There ain't nothin' the matter with us, mister. Sick! Ah'd like youn to show me whar we have any sick people."

Prejudice, blatant and subtle, was the real reason behind the desire to exclude Blacks. Petitions protesting black immigration were circulated throughout Edmonton in the spring of 1911. A head tax of one thousand dollars for each Black was demanded. Mr. Fisher, Secretary of the Board of Trade said, "Ninety per cent of the citizens who have been asked to sign the petitions against the negro immigration have compiled without hesitation." The petition was actually signed by more than 3400 people — approximately seven per cent of the city's population. Other resolutions were sent by citizens of Fort Saskatchewan, Strathcona, and Yorkton.

The local colony of Blacks was up in arms against the petitions: "Whenever a request for signature was made, a coloured man was ready to intervene, with apparently little effort." Mr. Fisher suggested that the Blacks were "very foolish" to oppose the petitions. Nevertheless, they did. The *Edmonton Daily Bulletin* reported: "One canvasser's steps were dogged by several negroes who intruded into the conversation and canvassed and sought to dissuade the latter from signing." The downtown offices of Watson Realty, Union Bank, Windsor Hotel, King Edward Hotel, Merchants' Bank, and the Board of Trade rooms displayed the petition. The petition, sent to Prime Minister Laurier, is presented here in full:

> We, the undersigned residents of the city of Edmonton, respectfully urge upon your attention and upon that of the Government of which you are the head, the serious menace to the future welfare of a large portion of Western Canada, by reason of the alarming influx of negro settlers. This influx commenced about four years ago in a very small way, only four or five families coming in the first season, followed by thirty

80

or forty families the next year. Last year several hundred negroes arrived in Edmonton and settled in surrounding territory. Already this season nearly three hundred have arrived; and the statement is made, both by these arrivals and by press dispatches, that these are but the advance guard of hosts to follow. We submit that the advent of such negroes as are now here was most unfortunate for the country, and that further arrivals in large numbers would be disastrous. We cannot admit as any factors the argument that these people may be good farmers or good citizens. It is a matter of common knowledge that it has been proved in the United States that negroes and whites cannot live in proximity without the occurrence of revolting lawlessness and the development of bitter race hatred, and that the most serious question facing the United States today is the negro problem. We are anxious that such a problem should not be introduced into this lawlessness as have developed in all sections in the United States where there is any considerable negro element. There is not reason to believe that we have here a higher order of civilization, or that the introduction of a negro problem here would have different results. We therefore respectfully urge that such steps immediately be taken by the Government of Canada as will prevent any further immigration of negroes into Western Canada. And your petitioners, as in duty bound, will ever pray.

Edmonton Capital, April 25, 1911

Premier Sifton said that no law existed that could keep Blacks out of the province. But protests continued. A large number of women railed against such a "short sighted policy". Dr. Ella Synge, spokeswoman for the group, said that "surely the result of Lord Gladstone's foolishness in South Africa is apparent enough already, in the enormous increase in outrages on white women that has occurred." She warned that

the finger of fate is pointing to lynch law which will be the ultimate result, as sure as we allow such people to settle among us.

Edmonton Capital, March 27, 1911

In a 1911 speech to a large Conservative Club audience Mr. C. E. Simmons of Lethbridge condemned the Liberal government for allowing Blacks to settle in the area. The *Edmonton Journal* reported his speech in an item titled "We Want No Dark Spots in Alberta". It was noted that Simmons' remarks were greatly enjoyed and appreciated by the audience.

Business agent McRogers and Secretary A. Von Ruyven of Edmonton's Hotel and Restaurant Employees Union issued a policy which demanded only white labour in the city's hotels. Edmonton's bartenders entered the picture. One newspaper reported:

> Irate Negroes were turned down services in two hotels. They ask, "Have Edmonton bartenders the right to draw the colour line?" The attorney-general's department said while it gives the hotel keeper the right to sell liquor, "it cannot compel him to sell to anyone if he does not wish to do so". All this in spite Negroes were "togged out" in the most fashionable of American clothes, almost dandified in their get-up and bearing.

Edmonton Capital, April 9, 1912

Even the sports page of the day told of such prejudice. A 1910 *Edmonton Daily Bulletin* article titled "Alleged Negro Has Been Declared Ineligible to Play in Western Canada League" told of an "alleged" Black named Brookins who was declared ineligible to play baseball for Regina against the Medicine Hat team. Brookins did play in the tournament and league President Eckstrom awarded the game to Medicine Hat by "default" because of Brookins' "ineligibility" — although Regina won the game!

Attempts to keep the Blacks out of Alberta and out of Canada became a political "hot potato". As the *Toronto Mail and Empire* reported: "Negro Immigrant Influx Has Become Live Issue". The next day that paper printed the following editorial:

> If negroes and white people cannot live in accord in the South, they cannot live in accord in the North.

Our Western population is being recruited largely by
white people from the United States. If freely admit
black people from that country, we shall soon have
the race troubles that are the blot on the civilization of
our neighbours. Canada cannot be accused of nar-
rowness if she refuses to open up her west to waves
of negro immigrants from the United States. The
negro question is of the United States' own making
and Canada should not allow any part of her territory
to be used as a relief colony on that account.

Toronto Mail and Empire, April 28, 1911

Anti-Black personnel such as W. R. Rennison of Athabaska
Landing were appointed immigration officers. A 1911 issue of
The Northern News of Athabaska Landing optimistically printed
this headline: "Canada Will Keep the Negro Out". Plans of the
federal government to adopt restrictive measures against the
migration of Blacks was the subject of a Winnipeg conference in
April of 1911, between Assistant Secretary of State Wilson and
John E. Jones, Consul-General of the United States. The 1910
Canadian immigration law had made immigration "restricted,
exclusive, and selective," but had not officially barred any
particular group of people. The reciprocity issue made even
more delicate any discussion with the United States of Black
immigration. American Blacks were not pleased with the
Canadian immigration policies. The militant W. E. B. DuBois,
black editor of *Crisis*, the organ of the National Association for
the Advancement of Coloured People, demanded explanations.
L. M. Fortier of the Canadian immigration department responded in typical manner:

There is nothing in the Canadian Immigration law
which bars any person on the ground of colour, but
since coloured people are not considered as a class
likely to do well in this country all other regulations
respecting health, money, etc., are strictly enforced
and it is quite possible that a number of your fellow
countrymen may be rejected on such grounds.

Crisis, Vol. 1, April 11, 1911

Newspapers warned the Ottawa government of a potential

Canadian "race problem". The *Edmonton Daily Bulletin*, for instance, observed that the negro's "presence in southern states had led to certain conditions" and "it is feared that his coming here in large numbers might lead to like condition". An Ottawa dispatch added:

> Frank Oliver, Minister of the Interior, has a difficult task on his hands if he has any hopes of securing Opposition approval of his immigration policy . . . Today in the Commons Mr. Thoburn of Lanark led them in a second attack because the department had admitted a number of negroes to settlement in the west, despite the fact that their colour and experience in the southern States made them objectionable.
>
> *The Globe* (Toronto) — April 4, 1911

The House of Commons debate continued with the Honourable Mr. Thoburn addressing Mr. Oliver: "The opinion is freely offered that steps should be taken by the Dominion Government to put a stop to a class of immigration that the experience of the southern states would indicate is hardly to be considered to be desirable". A further question by Mr. Thoburn was ruled out of order by the speaker but the next day he raised the issue again when he asked the House: "Would it not be preferable to preserve for the sons of Canada the lands they propose to give to niggers?" Strong words! In spite of Thoburn's rhetoric the law remained unchanged.

By 1911 the Canadian border was almost closed to Blacks as a result of the virtual surrender of the Immigration Branch to citizen demands. The colour line was drawn by public opinion rather than by government policy.

What news "The Black 1000" made! What writing they inspired! This is especially significant when their numbers are considered in perspective. Between 1901 and 1912 more than two million immigrants had come to Canada. Of these, 608,965 came to Alberta and Saskatchewan. Fewer than one in six hundred, then, were black.

Of the two million new immigrants to Canada 700,000 were American. In 1909 K. S. Hayes, writing in the *Busy Man's Magazine* observed that "the American has the heart of the Viking — once they conquered by the sword, but now they are conquering by the plow-share." That there was anti-American sentiment in Ottawa and in the West can not be disputed. However, anti-Black sentiment was not simply anti-American sentiment. Americans brought their own prejudices with them and these included anti-Black prejudice. Blacks were not considered a natural part of the Canadian scheme of things. Nor were they simply Americans. They were black.

Colour separates. Colour labels. Colour fathers colour. Where the second and third generation Hungarian, for example, may be identified as a "Hungarian-Canadian" or a "Canadian of Hungarian descent", the second or third generation Canadian Black remains just that — black.

Ten years after Western Canadian doors were unofficially closed to Blacks, Clifford Sifton reflected on the tremendous immigration he had encouraged during the Laurier years (1986-1911). In his speech to the Toronto Board of Trade the former Minister of the Interior made his now famous statement: "I think a stalwart peasant in a sheepskin coat, born on the sail, whose forefathers have been farmers for ten generations, with a stout wife and a half-dozen children, is good quality." It was clear that black Americans were not "good quality" — they were out of place in what was to be, after all, white man's country.

Black Amber

The black farmers of Amber Valley worked hard to prosper in a new land. Many of them took winter jobs on the railroads and in logging and freighting in order to increase livestock holdings, make farm improvements, and provide extra dietary items. Supplies were carried from Athabasca on a regular basis.

The experience of subsequent decades of Amber Valley farmers is encouraging, indicating as it does that perhaps only knowledge of another racial, ethnic, cultural, or religious group is needed in order to understand and accept. In 1949 one Amber Valley Black spoke of the group's acceptance by the community: "We only know we are of a different colour when we look in a mirror."

In 1977 Jefferson Davis Edwards reminisced:

A bunch of us got together and started to move from

Oklahoma. We had a taste of freedom and did not want to lose it.

He was proud of the Amber Valley Blacks' accomplishments:

When we came here, you couldn't see a hundred yards for timber and today from seventy-five to one hundred acres are broken on every quarter.

And he was proud to be considered "one of the leading coloured folk of Canada" — a reference to his listing in *Black Tiles in the Mosaic*, a calendar of highlights of the black experience in Canada. "The land is good," he said, looking out over the valley. His life on the Canadian prairies had brought peace and serenity.

THE BLACK MIRROR

The dream of a homogenized people had been heralded by Emerson in 1845. The experience of black pioneers on the Canadian prairies proved at least one thing: the melting pot concept was false, or, in any case, not workable in Canada.

It must be remembered, however, that western Whites' reactions to Blacks should not be viewed in isolation. The "black presence" brought displeasure to Canadians in all parts of the country. In Saint John, all restaurants and theatres closed their doors to Blacks in 1915. In Halifax, Fredericton, and Colchester, Blacks could not be buried in Anglican churchyards. A St. Croix, Nova Scotia by-law passed in 1907, read: "Not any Negro or coloured person nor any Indian shall be buried in St. Croix cemetery." As late as 1968 the by-law was cited to prevent the burial of a black child in the cemetery. In Bathurst, New Brunswick, a group of Whites spread the word that a by-law required all Blacks to leave town by nightfall. In Nova Scotia's Pictou County Blacks were not permitted to live in Stellarton, Westville, Trenton, or Pictou itself. In Truro a white vigilante group ordered Blacks off the streets at night. In 1937 a black man purchased a home in a white section of Trenton, Nova Scotia. A large mob of Whites stoned the man and "raided" his house. During World War II Blacks worked on the Alaska Highway project in segregated units. In 1957 Maurice Reddick, the black hero of the Springhill mine disaster, was not allowed to join the local "white" legion.

Meanwhile, the Ku Klux Klan (KKK) had entered Canada in the 1920s. Its publication, the Kourier Magazine, used its racist sloganeering to attack Blacks, Catholics, and Jews as well as to warn Canada of the Red Scare (Communism). Any people who could not be assimilated easily into a white protestant milieu were to be excluded from "Kanada". The Klan had a degree of acceptance in Moose Jaw, Saskatchewan where nearly 8,000 people attended its organizational meeting. The KKK became unfortunately and unfairly linked with that province's Conservative party led by Dr. J.T.M. Anderson. In 1929, C.S. Davis, a Liberal candidate for Prince Albert, falsely claimed that Conservative John George Diefenbaker was co-operating with the KKK. In the end, the Conservatives won the election and the Klan lost its support. That some of the Klan's leaders "skipped town" with the group's monies did little to enhance "the buffoons in nightgowns". Perhaps 19,000 Westerners had supported the organization's stress of separation of church and state, "patriotism", and the one public school concept. Of course, blood "purity" was central to the Klan's platform. "Niggers" were objects to be dismissed. Perhaps the activities of the KKK in Canada have been more laughable than dangerous. In 1976, this writer spoke with the leader of a branch of the Klan in Alberta. His intentions were questionable if not absurd.

The "Black 1000" which came to Alberta and Saskatchewan between 1908 and 1911 came to escape experiences they had had in Kansas, Oklahoma and elsewhere. They believed that there would be less prejudice, greater job opportunity, and a happier life in Canada. They came to escape Jim Crow laws and "grandfather clauses" which prevented them from casting their ballots. The group was part of a great northern movement of

Blacks from the South. It is important to note that they came as a group and not as individuals. Nearly 300 of those Blacks went to Amber Valley alone, where they sought a collective identity and comfort. "The black horde" clearly brought out the latent racism of white settlers who could accept individual Blacks such as Ware and Shadd — men who had the stuff from which heroes are made. The larger group helped to change Whites' attitudes in one respect; Blacks no longer could be considered mere isolated and romantic curiosities.

The mistakes or crimes of lone Blacks resulted in the description of all Blacks as treacherous, crafty, superstitious, brutish, lazy, child-like and ignorant. To this conventional wisdom Canadians added doctrines of their own: Blacks could not survive the Canadian climate, they were an economic drag on the community, their sexual proclivities made them dangerous.

Black prostitutes were even more horrifying than their red, white and yellow sisters. In 1901 there were nearly 30,000 more males than females in a prairie population of 427,254. By 1911 the situation had become more desperate for the men: they outnumbered women by nearly 200,000. Prostitution, then, became a social issue. The "oldest profession" has always been open to people of all races. But the existence of Blacks who were also "scarlet" disgusted many on a white Canadian frontier.

While it is true that Blacks on the prairies experienced a peculiar mixture of white hostility, apathy and indifference, they also had other problems. They had a lack of unity within a province or the cumulative pride that the list of individual acts of defiance would lead the observer to expect. Separated by geography and differing histories they remained one generation behind their American brothers in terms of expressing their demands. They followed the Gradualist, Accommodationist philosophy of Booker T. Washington, rather than the more militant W.E.B. DuBois attitude. Many engaged in an "Over there" type of thinking which suggested to them that Blacks elsewhere were in a more difficult position, and therefore that prairie Blacks had that much less to complain about. And they had few black heroes for their children. Could they identify with Josiah Henson, the so-called "Uncle Tom"?

Between 1880 and 1920 it became clear that in many Canadian

Blacks, White society had ingrained deep feelings of inferiority, complemented by equally pronounced feelings of inadequacy. Whites and their institutions had created racism, maintained it and largely condoned it. The result of the psychology of white racial supremacy had been a corresponding psychology of black inferiority. Few Blacks managed to escape it (Shadd and Ware were two exceptions to that rule). Viewed in extreme and colour aside, Blacks attempted to achieve one of two incompatible goals — survival as a distinct ethnic group, or admittance into the mainstream of Canadian life. Their faith in Canadian cultural pluralism caused them to believe that choice possible. However, that identity or "we-groupness" could not be established by either ignoring white racism or by withdrawing into any kind of isolation. Perhaps the racial climate in Canada called for a Black-White dialogue and confrontation which could have served to undercut those who would legitimize violence. Surely the Blacks' clear definition of demands and problems could have led to clearer self-identity. Surely their principal concerns should not have been tolerance or intolerance, but rather respect or contempt by the majority race. And their search for civil rights should have ended with equality but with self-respect if the former term means sameness. It would be an over-simplification to suggest that their reasons lay in the long-standing view that respectability was possible for Blacks only if they emphasized those characteristics which were non-Black.

The Black status between 1880 and 1920 perhaps more closely resembled the defining properties of caste rather than class. Blacks tended to retain throughout their lives a lowly position in the social structure into which they were born — their social mobility blocked by their white neighbours' commitment to the *status quo*. The historic powerlessness of Canadian Blacks was maintained by their exclusion from positions of authority in White-controlled institutions, and by the narrowly hemming-in of Blacks' churches and schools.

Prairie Blacks, in particular, lacked leadership from within their own group. That lack of leadership helped to shape the white image of the submissive, obsequious, imitative black man. Indeed, one must doubt that the following, more recent comment by a Canadian Black could have been made by an early Black on the Western Canadian frontier:

I am a Black (with a capital B). . . . I harbour no
inferiority complexes about my beautiful Blackness.
'Negro' is a polite way of saying 'nigger'. I am no
Negro, nor am I coloured; for Black is an absence of
colour. I am a Black Canadian; I'm Black and I'm
proud.

> The Chronicle-Herald, (Halifax),
> December 16, 1968,
> Letter to the Editor

Black may be beautiful, but that slogan scarcely could have
contributed to an understanding by Whites.

Historically, the prospect of the intermarriage of Blacks and
Whites has held more terror for the dominant white Canadian
society than any single feature of the Blacks. This is especially
true when applied to the instance of a black man's marriage to a
white woman. Dr. Shadd's marriage in Melfort, Saskatchewan,
was unusual in that respect. A black woman's marriage to a
white man has usually caused far less outrage perhaps because
of the husband's previously unquestioned role as "head" of the
North American family.

Although lacking in organization Canadian Blacks have often
displayed tenacity and fortitude in the face of racism. At the
Emerson, Manitoba border-crossing where they were subjected
to demeaning physical examinations numerous Blacks let their
displeasure be known. Other Blacks dogged the footsteps of the
white Edmontonians who demanded by petition that black
people be denied entry into Alberta. And in March, 1911 a black
porter of the Canadian National Railway sent a careful report to
Ottawa officials outlining the accomplishments of Blacks in the
Southern United States. The petition clearly identified black
gains in the fields of education, finance, and agriculture.

Still other Blacks considered the possibility of following the
Marcus Garvey movement — the idea of North American Blacks
returning to Africa. The movement gained relatively little
support in the United States and even less support in Canada.
Canadians had earlier considered and rejected such a movement. An 1890 issue of *The Week,* a Toronto journal, had this to
say:

But any partial movement of this kind, which would

91

suffice simply to drain off the most energetic and enterprising part of the coloured population, would but intensify the evils and make the last state of the mass remaining behind worse than the first.

In Edmonton, spokesmen for the "Black 1000" were quick to point out that they had been successful farmers in Oklahoma and Kansas. They were proud of their families and optimistic about their future. They felt that they had something to offer Canada. They did not come merely to receive. Some Blacks tore down "White Only" signs on restaurants and other public buildings. Noted earlier was the story of John Ware who bodily threw a white, racist tormentor into the street, and the head-on arguments of Alfred Shadd — arguments with white medical students, colleagues, electors, politicians, and hospital board members. Years earlier, a man who had many and strange versions of reality, Daniel Williams, presented himself as a man with whom few men, white or black, would or could argue. Here was a man who sought his own reality in his own turmoil, and who staggered alone through a separate darkness somewhere between melancholy and contempt. Black men like David "Sixapekwan" Mills made their statements with their hard work. These few instances support the claim that Sambo was a white invention rather than a black reality.

The black criminal found his world made of glass windows. "Nigger Dan" Williams, for instance, helped to show the "true colour" of the white frontier's racial attitudes. Williams, a man whose malice could always find a mark to shoot at and a pretense to fire, provided "proof" of black criminality. Similarly, the actions of William Bond only buttressed the commonly-accepted idea that the criminal streak ran through all Blacks.

Where a black suspect was involved, the code of "innocent until proven guilty" often worked in reverse. Jesse Williams' was a case in point. Even before his trial began, the local newspaper reported in full "A Negro's Terrible Crime" and added that "no doubt he will tell the whole truth before he 'swings off' ".

Whites were slow to evaluate the lives of men such as John Ware, Doc Shadd, or David Mills — powerful people in a difficult time and place. Their characteristics were not transferred to the black caricature. Only "bad niggers" supported the stereotype. Blacks such as Shadd, Ware, and Jefferson Davis Edwards were not seen as typical of their colour.

The white pioneer who claimed to "work like a nigger" all week and who said that all Blacks "look the same to me" may have unknowingly stated a strange truth: many Blacks did wear masks which hid their true feelings. The young black poet, Paul Laurence Dunbar (1872-1906) expresses that idea in his poem, "We Wear the Mask":

> We wear the mask that grins and lies,
> It hides our cheeks and shades our eyes,
> This debt we pay to human guile;
> With torn and bleeding hearts we smile,
> And mouth with myriad subtleties.
>
> Why should the world be overwise,
> In counting all our tears and sighs?
> Nay, let them only see us, while
>   We wear the mask.
>
> We smile, but, O great Christ, our cries
> To thee from tortured souls arise.
> We sing, but oh, the clay is vile
> Beneath our feet, and long the mile;
> But let the world dream otherwise,
>   We wear the mask.

Today, that mask is being removed. Black pride is sweeping North America — justifiable pride in black culture and history. In many instances, anger also emerges from under the mask. Reasons for that anger can be found, in part, in the experiences of pioneer Blacks in Canada.

The black mirror reflects an unhappy image. Indeed, the history of Blacks in Canada is sad because of what it reveals about a wider society's values. But, perhaps consideration of that history can bring about positive results. Perhaps it can prompt that society to examine and evaluate its attitudes and actions so that the injustices of the past might not be perpetrated in the future, so that all the peoples of this nation might live and work together peacefully in a fellowship of understanding and mutual respect.

CHRONOLOGY OF
BLACKS IN CANADA

1492 A Black, Pedro Alonso Nino, accompanies Columbus to America. Later, other Blacks serve under Balboa, Ponce de Leon, Cortez, Menendes, Lewis and Clark and others.

1608 Mathieu d'Acosta, a Black, serves as interpreter for Sieur de Monts, Governor at Port Royal, the French outpost established in what is now Nova Scotia. A Christian, d'Acosta was a member of Canada's oldest club, The Order of Good Cheer.

1619 A "Dutch manne of Warre" trades twenty black slaves for food at Jamestown, Virginia. Today, the incident is seen by many as the beginning of black slavery in North America.

1628 A black slave from Madagascar is sold in New France by one David Kirke. It is Canada's first recorded slave sale. The boy slave's original name is discarded in favour of "Olivier Le Jeune" (after his teacher, Paul Le Jeune, a

Jesuit missionary). In 1632, Olivier is given to a friend of Champlain's. (In 17th century New France black slavery was illegal and there was very limited direct slave trade with Africa.)

1685 The *Code Noir* and its 1724 revision are claimed to have applicability to New France. Part of the code states that slaves are chattels (meubles) to be owned by their masters.

1688 Because of a shortage-of labour in French Canada, Louis XIV is asked to allow black slavery in the colony. Governor Denonville eventually receives the king's permission. At the time, there are numerous Panis (Indian) slaves in New France.

1689 Louis XIV receives an official suggestion from New France noting that black slavery could be profitable.

1689-
1709 In this twenty-year period the legal foundation for slavery in New France is established by a series of decrees.

1705 A New York law prescribes the prompt execution of black slaves who have escaped from their masters.

1709 Slavery is declared legal in New France. Intendant Jacques Raudot's ordinance clearly notes that black slaves can be bought and sold.

1734 Gilles Hocquart, Intendant, attempts to discourage the escape of slaves from New France.

1759 Battle of the Plains of Abraham

1760 The 47th Article of Capitulation allows slavery to continue under British rule. General James Murray, Governor of Quebec, expresses the wish that more black slaves could be imported. At the time, there are approximately 4,000 slaves — Black and Indian — in Quebec.

1766 Ten percent of the 30,000 United Empire Loyalists who come to Canada during and after the American War of Independence are Blacks — free and enslaved.

1777 Canadian slaves escape to Vermont where slavery has been abolished.

1781 The government of Prince Edward Island declares that conversion to Christianity does not free a Black from slavery.

1783 General George Washington meets with Guy Carleton in an unsuccessful attempt to stop Blacks from escaping into

British lines. One group of soldiers, The Black Pioneers, serves the British forces with distinction. After the American War of Independence, many of them come to the Maritimes where they fail to receive land grants equal to those offered to other Empire soldiers.

Quakers in New Brunswick, Nova Scotia, and other regions of Canada fight against slavery.

Over 3,000 Blacks, free and enslaved, arrived with the United Empire Loyalists. (Today, some of their descendants proudly write U.E.L. after their names.)

1784 A large number of slaves are baptized in St. Paul's Church, Halifax.

In and near Montreal there are 304 black slaves.

In Birchtown (near Shelburne) Nova Scotia, a mob of angry Whites (many of them disbanded soldiers) destroy Blacks' homes. They argue that some of Birchtown's 1500 Blacks have taken their jobs by accepting smaller wages. The near-riot is one of Canada's most ugly racial incidents.

1787 Canadian slaves escape to parts of the United States where slavery has been outlawed.

1789 Josiah Henson (the model for "Uncle Tom" in Harriet Beecher Stowe's *Uncle Tom's Cabin*) is born a Maryland slave.

1791 Upper and Lower Canada are created by the Constitutional Act. An estimated 325 slaves live in Upper Canada at the time.

1792 1,200 free Blacks leave Nova Scotia and New Brunswick for Sierra Leone, Africa.

1793 The Legislature of Upper Canada abolishes slavery.

1796 The Society for the Propagation of the Gospel in Foreign Parts (SPG), an Anglican organization formed in 1701, begins the organized education of Blacks in Canada. (These efforts were centred in the Maritimes.)

1797 Emmanuel Allen, a slave, is sold in Montreal.

1797 Scipio, a black youth, is sold in New Brunswick. His sale is one of the last in that province.

1800 400 Maroons, who had arrived in Halifax four years earlier from Jamaica, are transported to Sierra Leone, Africa. (Some of the older Maroons had earlier been stolen from their African homes and transplanted in America.)

A separate cemetery for Blacks is opened in Montreal.

Robin, a black slave, is freed by a Quebec court. With this manumission slavery effectively ends in Quebec.

1803 Pierre Bongo, a Black, serves the North West Company at the Pembina River fort.

1813 A black corps helps to defend Fort George during the War of 1812.

1813-
1816 Approximatley 2,000 Blacks (refugees of the War of 1812) arrive in the Maritimes.

1816 The last known advertisement for a runaway slave to appear in a Canadian newspaper is printed in New Brunswick's *Royal Gazette*, July 10, 1816.

1818 Black voyageur, Grand Michel serves the Hudson's Bay Company in the Peace River district.

1819 Crawford Glasgow, a Black, serves the Hudson's Bay Company in the Athabasca region (northern Alberta).

1820 In St. John, New Brunswick, a school for Blacks is declared a success.

1821 95 Black Refugees of the War of 1812 leave Canada for Trinidad in the schooner *William*. (Most of these had settled near Beech Hill, Nova Scotia.)

1823 Mifflin W. Gibbs, black businessman, statesman, judge and strong supporter of Canadian confederation, is born in Philadelphia. In 1858, he leads a group of Blacks to Canada's West Coast.

1824 1,200 Blacks leave for Canada after a race riot in Cincinnati, Ohio.

1832 The Second Convention of People of Color meets in Philadelphia and plans to buy land in Canada for Blacks "who may be, by oppressive enactments, obliged to flee from these United States".

1833 Slavery is outlawed in the British Empire.

1837 Some Canadian Blacks (male only) enfranchised.

Twelve-year-old Maria Walker is an indentured servant for a white man in New Brunswick.

Josiah Henson leads the second company of "Essex coloured volunteers" in the defense of Ford Malden (Amherstburg) from December, 1837 to May, 1838. In January, 1838 he helps to capture the American schooner

Anne. These actions take place during the 1837-38 rebell-
ions in Upper and Lower Canada.

Anderson R. Abbott, black surgeon, soldier, poet, and
educator, is born in Toronto.

1839 Canadian Blacks are allowed to sit on juries.

1841 The Dawn Settlement in Canada West is begun with the
purchase of parcels of land.

1842 69 fugitive slaves are conveyed across Lake Erie to Canada
by William Welles Brown, a black steamboat captain and
former slave. (This item is representative of many similar
slave escapes into Canada.)

Nelson Hackett, a fugitive slave, is deported to the United
States. Hackett's deportation is unique amongst escaped
slaves.

1846 Superintendent of Education, Egerton Ryerson receives
notice from Amherstburg School Trustees (Canada West)
that white residents there, rather than send their children
"to school with niggers" will "cut their children's heads off
and throw them into the roadside ditch".

Near Amherstburg nearly 10,000 acres of land are set aside
for the Refugee Home Settlement for Blacks.

1849 Rival Irish groups, quarrelling while working on the
Welland Canal, are "separated" by black troops.

1850 Canada West's Separate School Act allows for *de facto*
segregated schools. (Much gerrymandering of school
district boundaries strengthened the segregated school
concept.)

The American Fugitive Slave Bill of 1850 acts as a catalyst
in the formation of anti-slavery societies in Canada.

1851 The Canada Anti-Slavery Society holds its first meeting in
Toronto.

In St. Catharines, Harriet Tubman, "The Moses of her
People", begins her work with the Underground Railroad.
For seven years she will guide fugitive slaves into Canada.

1852 Harriet Beecher Stowe's *Uncle Tom's Cabin* is published in
Toronto and Montreal.

1853 *The Provincial Freeman*, perhaps Canada's best-known
"black" newspaper, is begun in Windsor, Canada West.
For a time, Mary Ann Shadd will be employed by the
paper.

1854 Mary Ann Shadd, writing in *The Provincial Freeman*, opposes the ideas expressed in Henry Bibb's *Voice of the Fugitive*.

1858 A black doctor in Chatham, Canada West, Martin R. Delaney, tries unsuccessfully to encourage Canadian Blacks to migrate to Africa. His plan, involving the Niger Valley Exploring Party, will be paralleled in 1859 by the efforts of Nova Scotia's Edward Blyden. (Better known is the American Black Marcus Garvey's back-to-Africa movement which was considered by Canadian Blacks in the 1920s.)

In May of this year, John Brown meets in Chatham with Blacks and sympathetic Whites to plan his move against slavery in the United States. A year later, he will make his famous raid on Harper's Ferry, Virginia.

A party of California Blacks prepare to leave for Canada's West Coast.

1859 Abraham D. Shadd is elected to the Raleigh (Canada West) town council. It is the first time a Canadian Black is elected to public office.

Canada West school legislation (which will remain to 1964) allows for legally segregated schools. (In 1964, Leonard A. Braithwaite, black Member of the Legislature for Etobicoke, Ontario, spoke out against the long-standing legislation. In Ontario, a number of mid-19th-century court cases had severely weakened the segregation plan. In Amber Valley, Alberta, an all-Black school existed until the early 1960s. Residentially segregated schools still exist today in Nova Scotia.)

In Toronto, a memorial service is held for the hanged John Brown. Blacks contribute money which is given to Brown's widow.

1859-
1864 In 1859, the first of an estimated 600 Blacks arrive on Vancouver Island. One of the group's leaders, Mifflin W. Gibbs, becomes a very successful businessman in Victoria where he is elected to city council. Other Blacks participate in the Cariboo Gold Rush. Numerous Blacks settle on Salt Spring Island.

1860 By this time, at least 500 Canadian Blacks have travelled to the Deep South to help to free their brothers and sisters.

1861 In Victoria, British Columbia, the all-Black Pioneer Rifle Corps receives recognition.

Anderson Ruffin Abbott becomes the first Canadian-born black graduate of a medical college (University of Toronto). The 1850 American Fugitive Slave Bill has increased the black migration to Canada. In the decade from 1851 to 1861 New Brunswick's black population doubles to nearly 1,600. By 1861 Nova Scotia's 6,000 Blacks accound for 2% of the Nova Scotia population. Canada West's black population rises by 3,000 to an 1861 total of more than 11,000. In the same year, there are approximately 600 Blacks on Canada's West Coast. In Canada East, there are fewer than 200 Blacks.

1901 The black population of Canada is 17,437. Haitians and Jamaicans are not included in this census figure.

1902 William Hall, black Canadian war hero and the first black recipient of the Victoria Cross, is buried in an unmarked Canadian grave.

British Columbia's Mifflin Gibbs publishes an autobiography, *Shadow and Light*. Additional papers are to follow; 1923 *The Dawn of Tomorrow*, a newspaper, is published in London, Ontario; in 1934, *The Free Lance* begins publication in Montreal; in 1946, Mrs. Carrie Best of New Glasgow, Nova Scotia, publishes *The Clarion*. A number of other black newspapers follow and are short-lived. Perhaps the best known of these is *The Canadian Negro* published from 1953 to 1956. Recent black Canadian newspapers and magazines include *Contrasts*, *Uhuru*, *The Black Voice* and *Talking Drums*. In 1973, Austin Clarke, one of Canada's best black writers, publishes *Storm of Fortune*.

1904 Birth of Charles Drew, black Canadian doctor, and discoverer of a process for the storing of blood plasma.

1905 W.E.B. DuBois, black American leader and writer, calls black leaders to Niagara Falls, Ontario. The "Niagara Movement" demands equality for Blacks in education, employment, justice and other areas. Their Declaration of Principles demands political and social justice for all Blacks. The movememt later gives rise to the National Association for the Advancement of Coloured People

(NAACP). DuBois opposes Booker T. Washington's Accomodationist, work-ethic point of view.

In Melfort, Saskatchewan, Alfred S. Shadd, by a few votes, loses the distinction of being the first Black to be elected to a Canadian provincial legislature.

Cowboy John Ware dies.

1908-
1911 Approximately 1,000 Blacks, mostly from Oklahoma, arrive on the Canadian Prairies.

1909 Matthew Henson, a Black, co-discovers the North Pole.

1910 Life expectancy for North American Blacks is reported to be 34 years for males and 38 years for females.

1911 The issue of "land for the niggers" is debated in the Canadian House of Commons.

Petitions are sent to Ottawa from Winnipeg, Edmonton and Calgary demanding that the federal government stop the movement of Blacks into the Prairies.

There is a reported "negro lynching" on the average of once every six days in North America.

1912 Dr. William Pearly Oliver, black Canadian civil rights leader, clergyman, educator, writer and a founder of the Nova Scotia Association for the Advancement of Coloured People (NSAAC), and the Black United Front (BUF), is born in Wolfville, Nova Scotia.

1914 Blacks in St. John, New Brunswick are refused admission to theatres and some bars.

Blacks are among the first Canadian soldiers to leave for World War I.

1914-
1918 Canadian Blacks serve in both segregated and non-segregated army units overseas. James Grant, an Ontario Black, receives the Military Cross for bravery in action. Numerous black organizations across Canada raise money and provide supplies for the war effort.

1915 Alfred S. Shadd dies.

The Negro Chapter of the Red Cross is organized in Montreal.

1915-
1916 Blacks in Fredericton and Halifax are not allowed to bury their dead in Anglican churchyards. (An earlier St. Croix,

Nova Scotia by-law had made the same stipulation.)

1919 In Truro, Nova Scotia, Blacks are attacked and beaten by white Canadian soldiers. (The attack had been precipitated by the establishment of a camp for black soldiers in Truro.) In Liverpool, England, white Canadian and British soldiers brawl with black Canadian soldiers.

1920 The Ku Klux Klan moves into Canada. Their efforts are concentrated in the four Western provinces and in Ontario. Preaching Anglo-Saxon blood "purity" and Christian piety, they slander Blacks, Jews, Catholics and immigrants from southern Europe. (KKK groups operating in Canada today note that their nocturnal cross-burning escapades have, for the most part, been replaced by an appeal to "reason, democracy and patriotism".)

By this time, most Canadian Blacks are in a worse socio-economic position than their Canadian-born grand-parents had been. Anti-Black sentiment in Canada is most intense during the first twenty years of this century.

1921 The Canadian Brotherhood of Railroad Employees (which includes many Blacks) is formed in Montreal.

Fom this date to his death in 1940, James A. R. Kinney leads the Nova Scotia Home for Coloured Children.

The first modern increase in the black population of Canada is noted. Illiteracy among Canadian Blacks is approximately 8.5% — fifteenth highest of the forty one groups studied. Approximately 7% of Canada's Blacks have intermarried with other races. On a percentage basis, more Blacks are in Canadian jails and penitentiaries than any other group. The infant mortality rate of 15.9% is fourth highest of all ethnic groups. Nearly 75% of Canadian Blacks are Canadian-born.

1923 The *Franklin vs. Evans* law case allows Blacks to be legally refused service in Canadian restaurants. A significant number of similar rulings will be made throughout the 1920s and 1930s.

1924 Militant Blacks led by James Jenkins of London, Ontario and J. W. Montgomery of Toronto form the Canadian League (later, Association) for the Advancement of Coloured People. Within two years, other Ontario branches are formed in Dresden, Brantford, Niagara Falls and

103

Toronto.

1927 When a Chatham Black is accused of rape, the presiding judge congratulates white men of the area for not having "lynched" the culprit.

1928 The Montreal community of St. Antoine is served by three black doctors.

1928

1929 The KKK is active in Saskatchewan and its politics. Young Saskatchewan Conservative John George Diefenbaker is falsely accused of assisting the Klan.

1930 The KKK parades openly in the streets of Oakville, Ontario. Nearly all Canadian newspapers scorn the Klan.
An American Black, George Baker, better known as "Father Divine", is supported by some Canadian Blacks. Baker, who calls himself God, establishes "Heavens" where Depression-racked people are able to purchase cheap meals.

1932 Richard B. Harrison, "De Lawd" (born near London, Canada West) begins to preach in Canada.
Toronto's Larry Gains, who helped to break boxing's colour bar, is announced "The Colored Heavyweight Champion of the World".

1937 In Trenton, Nova Scotia, a white mob stones a black man's home.
William Pearly Oliver begins his Halifax ministry.

1938 In Toronto, Marcus Garvey conducts the Eighth International Convention of the Negro Peoples of the World.

1940 A mob of Canadian soldiers storm the Calgary home of a black bandleader.

1941 63% of Canada's Blacks are urban dwellers.

1942 Many Blacks work on the construction of the highway from Dawson Creek to Big Delta, Alaska.

1944 Ontario passes the Racial Discrimination Act.

1944 Sylvia Stark, a former slave and long-time resident of Salt Spring Island, British Columbia, dies at the age of 106.

1945 Jackie Robinson, a Black, signs to play for the Montreal Royals football team.

1946 The Nova Scotia Association for the Advancement of Coloured People is formed.

1947 Prime Minister Mackenzie King announces that Canada

wants "a good type of immigrant" who can be easily integrated into Canadian society.

1949 In Nova Scotia, only nine Blacks graduate from University.

1951 Addie Aylestock becomes a minister — perhaps the first black woman in Canada to gain this distinction.

1952 Wilson Brooks becomes one of Toronto's first black teachers.

1953 Frederick Hubbard, black former chairman of the Toronto Transportation Commission, dies.

1954 "Separate but equal" education for Nova Scotia's black children exists in law to this date. (The 1918 Education Act allowed separate schools for Blacks.) By 1970, Blacks in Nova Scotia are to see much improvement in their educational opportunities. In Ontario, segregated schools are not to be legally abolished until 1964. In the 1950s and 1960s, racism is said to lead to the dismissal of black teachers in Wawota, Saskatchewan, Drumheller and Breton, Alberta, and parts of British Columbia and Nova Scotia.

Dresden, Ontario becomes the centre of bitter racial controversy when Blacks are refused service in public places.

1957 Ed Searles becomes one of British Columbia's first black lawyers.

1958 Maurice Reddick is a hero of the Spring Hill, Nova Scotia, mine disaster.

Cal Best becomes president of the 27,000-member Civil Service Association of Canada.

Willie O'Rea becomes first Black to play hockey in the N.H.L.

1959 Amherst's Donald Fairfax becomes the first Black to be appointed to the staff of the 200-year-old Nova Scotian Legislature.

The great-great-grandaughter of Josiah Henson, Mrs. Bruce Carter, places a wreath on the cenotaph honouring Blacks who defended Canada during the War of 1812.

1960 Significant numbers of West Indian Blacks begin to arrive in Canada.

1961 Jamaican premier, Norman Manley, attacks what he considers to be Canadian "colour bar". Trinidadian Prime

Minister, Eric Williams, and Barbados' Earl Barron criticize what they consider Canada's discrimination on trade and immigration policies.

Canadian government leads in exclusion of South Africa from the Commonwealth.

1962 Daniel G. Hill is appointed Director of the Ontario Human Rights Commission.

1963 W.E.B. DuBois dies in Ghana.

Ontario's Leonard Braithwaite becomes the first Black to be elected to a provincial legislature.

Many Canadian Blacks participate in the "March on Washington".

1964 W.P. Oliver receives Honourary Doctorate from King's College, Halifax.

Lincoln Alexander of Hamilton, Ontario becomes Canada's first black Member of Parliament.

1965 The KKK is said to be responsible for burning crosses in Amherstburg, Ontario. Spray paint on signs claim Amherstburg to be "Home of the KKK".

1967 The last of Halifax's Africaville homes is razed for the purpose of urban renewal.

1968 A Quebec Black receives court damages after he is refused the right to rent a home.

The annual Emancipation Celebration in Windsor, Ontario is banned.

Nova Scotia's St. Croix Cemetery refuses to allow the burial of a black child.

In Digby, Nova Scotia, a Black is jailed for five months for non-payment of taxes. Protests by Blacks and others lead to his release.

1969 Canada's first "Soul Food" restaurant, the "Underground Railroad" opens in Toronto.

Maurice Alexander Charles is made a provincial judge in Ontario.

Windsor Ontario's Patterson Collegiate institutes a Black Studies course.

The National Black Coalition of Canada is formed.

1970 There are more than 100,000 Blacks in Canada.

1971 Alberta's black population is estimated at 1,500.

Harry Jerome is awarded the medal of service "for

excellence in all fields of Canadian life".

1972 Montreal's first black congregation, Union United Church, celebrates its sixty-fifth anniversary.

Rosemary Brown becomes a member of the British Columbia Legislature.

Alberta's KKK is incorporated under the province's Society Act.

1973 Sylvester Campbell, ballet dancer, stars at O'Keefe Centre, Toronto.

Toronto's Clyde Grey is welterweight boxing champion of the Commonwealth.

Montreal's black population is estimated at 40,000. The majority of these are West Indian born.

1978 Folk-Rock star Dan Hill, son of Daniel G. Hill, wins three Juno awards.

Ontario Ministry of Education announces plans to make black Canadian history better known in the schools of Ontario.

INDEX

110